GREEK MYTHOLOGY

THE GODS OF OLYMPUS

Stephanides Brothers'

GREEK MYTHOLOGY

THE GODS OF OLYMPUS

☙

Retold by Menelaos Stephanides
Drowings by Yannis Stephanides

Translation
Bruce Walter

SIGMA

THE GODS OF OLYMPUS

First edition 1997, second edition 2001, third run 2005
Printed in Greece by "Fotolio-Typicon", bound by G. Betsoris
Copyright © 2001: Sigma Publications
All rights reserved throughout the world

SIGMA PUBLICATIONS
20, Mavromihali St., tel. +30 210 3607667, fax. +30 210 3638941
GR-106 80 ATHENS, GREECE
www.sigmabooks.gr, e-mail: sigma@sigmabooks.gr

ISBN: 960-425-058-2

A word on mythology

In the distant past, man was like a child that loves fairy tales. Virtually powerless against the forces of nature, he led a life of almost unimaginable difficulty and discomfort. All around him, awesome forces were at play, often bringing disaster upon his head, but sometimes dazzling him with their grandeur and filling him with a zest for life. In an effort to make this life less puzzling, he strove to find the causes underlying both the horrors and the joys he encountered in his daily existence. His pitifully limited knowledge, however, frustrated his attempts to find the true explanation for every phenomenon he encountered, and thus his imagination was set to work — a fertile imagination which wove incredible stories filled with beauty and rich in sentiment, but with a strong underlying vein of sorrow reflecting the arduous existence he led.

Thus myth was born – and hence mythology.

Since myths are filled with imaginary events, they seem to us today like fairy stories. They are not. Beneath these imaginary incidents some real event invariably lies concealed. In mythology can be found the very life itself of ancient peoples, but in the terms in which they themselves were able to see it or explain it; and above all can be found their vision of the nature of life and of the world. It was for this last reason, indeed, that the mythology of every ancient people was also its religion.

From the land of Greece sprang some of the loveliest myths of all the ancient peoples. The ancient Greeks wove their myths from the splendour of the Greek countryside and their love for life and for all that was beautiful.

They admired the heroes of those myths and worshipped the creatures of their fruitful imagination, the gods of Olympus. The final outcome of this was paradoxical: the immortal gods, who had had their existence in the minds of mortal men, eventually perished and their place was taken by the immortal works these men had created – Greek Mythology. Even today, it still teaches both young and old the meaning of goodness and beauty.

It is precisely this goodness and beauty, and the fairy-tale loveliness of Greek mythology that we have tried to convey in this series of illustrated books for children.

To what extent we have succeeded is for our readers, both young and old, to judge.

THE BIRTH OF THE WORLD

The world is created out of Chaos

This is a tale like no other you have ever heard. It begins in a time long, long ago, deeper in the past than any tale which has ever been told. To begin our story at its beginning we must go back countless centuries and move ever further backwards in time, searching for the beginning, the beginning of time which never was.

In that far distant age there lived, as there had always lived, a god named Chaos. He was all alone, and round him there was nothing but utter emptiness. In those times there was neither sun, nor light, nor earth, nor sky. There was nothing but a formless void and thick darkness stretching to infinity.

Untold centuries rolled by like this until, at last, Chaos grew tired of living by himself. It was then that he first thought of creating the world.

The first thing he did was to bring the goddess Earth into being. She was lovely beyond description; filled with strength and life, she grew and spread and enfolded huge expanses within her embrace. On her our world was founded.

Then Chaos created fearsome Tartarus and black Night, and straight after that the lovely and radiant Day.

The kingdom of Tartarus was deep and dark beyond imagining, as far within the earth as chaos was above it. If one dropped an iron anvil from that void it would go on falling for nine days and nine nights, and only at dawn on the tenth day would it reach the earth. And then, if it went on falling from the earth towards Tartarus, it would go on down for another nine days and nine nights and only on the morning of the tenth day would it reach those depths. That is how deep within the earth Tartarus lies, and that is why the darkness there is so thick and black. And Tartarus is boundless. If you entered it, you would move endlessly onwards, dragged on and buffeted by raging whirlwinds, and even in a year you would be unable to reach the far side.

In the heart of this frightful region, which even the immortal gods are afraid of, rise the dark courts of Night, forever wrapped in black clouds. Here Night sits all day, and when dusk falls, he spreads out over the earth.

Uranus ruler of the world

Now that Chaos had played his part, it was the turn of the goddess Earth to help in the creation of the world. She wished to begin with something beautiful, and so she gave birth to the goddess Love who brought the beauty of life to the world. Then she bore the boundless blue Sky, the Mountains and the Seas. All of them were mighty gods, but the greatest of them all was Uranus, the Sky. And so the goddess Earth, the mother of all things, bedecked and beautified the world and rejoiced in its creation.

Now, however, the mightiest god in the world was Uranus, who wrapped the earth in his blue mantle and covered it from edge to edge. He sat on his majestic golden throne borne up by clouds of many colours and from there he ruled the whole world and all the gods.

Uranus married the goddess Earth and she bore him many immortal children. Among them were the twelve Titans, six male and six female. The Titans were huge gods of fearsome power. Indeed, one of them, Oceanus, was so

huge that he spread out over the whole earth. He fathered
countless offspring. All the rivers upon earth were his
children and he had three thousand daughters, the Oceanides, who were the goddesses of springs and rivulets.

Another Titan, Hyperion, and his wife, the Titaness
Theia, brought three more lovely deities into being: the
bright Sun, rosy-fingered Dawn and the silvery Moon.

The last of the Titans was the crafty and ambitious Cronus; but of him we shall have more to say later.

Among the other children of Uranus and Earth were the
angry Cyclopes, huge gods with a single eye in the middle
of their foreheads. The Cyclopes had mastery over fire and
held sway over the thunder and lightning. They lived
among the high mountains, and on the summit of one they
had a fire which always burned, a huge volcano which they
used to forge weapons and armour. The Cyclopes were
creatures of awesome power, and when they moved among
the mountains, lightning flashes and claps of thunder shook
the earth and the whole world trembled at their passing.

But of all Uranus' children, the three largest and most
terrible were the Hundred-handed giants, creatures whose
strength was so great that they could hurl rocks as big as
mountains and make the whole world shake.

There were now many gods, but Uranus continued to
rule the world and keep order. His power was immense, his
every wish was law, and all obeyed his commands. The

years of Uranus' rule were happy ones, for in those days there were neither death, nor evil nor hatred.

But there is an end to all things.

One day, Uranus flew into a rage with his children, the Titans and the Hundred-handed giants. They had treated him with disrespect and so he decided to punish them severely. Earth, seeing his rage, knelt before him and begged him to forgive them.

"My lord," she cried. "Lord of the whole world; I beg you, forgive our children and do not bring disaster upon the family of the gods."

But the anger of Uranus was terrible to behold.

"Mother of the gods," he answered, "when children cease to respect their father they must be banished from the light of day. If I let them go unpunished they will challenge me again, and may even cast me down from the throne of the gods."

And with these words he opened the earth and hurled the Titans and the Hundred-handed giants into the dark depths of Tartarus where there is neither the light of day nor even the dim shade of night but thick, murky darkness without end.

Cronus casts Uranus from his throne

Uranus' wife was heartbroken to see the Titans confined

to the bowels of the earth; for were they not her children? She decided to speak to them and urge them to resist. "Alas," she said when she had found them. "How can I live for ever, knowing that my children are locked up in inky Tartarus? Which of you dares to become the new ruler of the gods? Your father has reigned for long enough. Now it is someone else's turn."

The Titans bent their heads, and so did the Hundred-handed giants. The power of Uranus was fearsome, and a hundred times more so when he was enraged. Not all the Titans were afraid, however. The eyes of one of them lit up with joy. This was Cronus, who had always longed to be lord of the world himself. He knew his father had made no mistake in casting them into Tartarus. But now, his turn had come.

With the help of his mother, Cronus escaped from his dark prison into the bright world of day. Unused to the light, his eyes were so dazzled that they could see nothing of the shining world which spread itself before them. But they soon grew used to the light, and then Cronus saw the fair earth with its high mountains, its broad blue seas and its boundless, light-filled skies, while the warmth of the sun fell like a gentle caress upon his body.

"Mother Earth," he cried, "thank you for letting me see this wonderful world again, this world which I will make my own. And now, farewell! I know the task which lies

...He slyly crept up on him and in a moment
the deed was done...

before me!"

And immediately, Cronus was lost to his mother's sight.
He fashioned a great sickle, wrapped himself in a cloud and
flew high in the sky, waiting for an opportunity to present
itself. It came just as he had wanted it. Finding Uranus
sleeping, he slyly crept up on him, and in a moment the
deed was done. He struck his father, wounded him horribly
and left him powerless – as powerless to rule the world
again as to father other children.

"A double success!" said Cronus to himself. "For now I
have nothing more to fear from Uranus." Scarcely had this
thought passed through his mind, however, when his
father's heavy curse came echoing like the roar of a wild
beast, whilst all nature darkened and thunder and lightning
shook the world.

"My curse upon you, misbegotten spawn – and what you
have done to your father may your own children do to
you!"

This was enough to freeze the blood in any veins, but it
left Cronus completely unconcerned. He was so overjoyed
by his success that he had no room in his mind for disturb-
ing thoughts. He released the other Titans from Tartarus,
and this gave him an even greater feeling of security, for on
them he could found his rule more firmly. But the Hundred-handed giants he left imprisoned, for he feared their
power, whilst he knew the Titans well and could always

use them to further his own interests. One Titan alone refused to help Cronus. This was Oceanus, who considered it so terrible for a son to wound his own father and seize his throne that he had no wish to be a party to Cronus' plans. And so he withdrew to the far corners of the world and lived in peace, wanting no share in his brother's unlawful rule.

However, the reign of Cronus, founded as it was upon such an evil deed, loosed a host of misfortunes upon the world. To punish Cronus, the goddess Night gave birth to a brood of fearsome deities such as Death and Fraud, Nightmares and Strife, vengeful Nemesis and a host of others. From his father's throne Cronus now ruled over a world filled with terror, cheating, hatred, anguish, vindictiveness and war. Now and ever after, both gods and men would pay for Cronus' sin.

The birth of Zeus

Even all-powerful Cronus himself was seized by a great fear. He was no longer certain that his rule would endure for ever. He now remembered his father's curse with horror and feared that his own children would rise against him as he had done against Uranus.

And so he took a horrible decision; he ordered his wife, Rhea, to bring him every child she bore, and each time that

she did so he would swallow it alive. In this way he consumed five infants which Rhea bore him: Hera, Demeter,
Hestia, Hades and Poseidon.

Rhea was now with child again, and she was at her wits'
end. She could not think what to do to save the infant. So
she went to her parents, Uranus and Mother Earth, who
advised her to have her baby in Crete, in a cave on Mount
Dicte, well hidden among the forests. In this sacred cave,
Rhea gave birth to her child and entrusted it to the nymphs
of the forest who had helped bring the baby into the world.
She then returned secretly to the palace of Cronus and
began to cry out that she had been seized by birth pangs.

The fearsome Cronus believed that his wife really was in
labour, and he did not fail to remind her once again of his
cruel orders: "Get it over with, woman, I can't bear your
screaming – and bring me the child immediately it is born."
And with these heartless words he left Rhea's room.

As soon as he had gone, Rhea took a stone, wrapped it in
cloth so that it could not be seen and a little later presented
it to her husband in place of the child. Cronus suspected
nothing, and swallowed the stone with satisfaction.

The baby that escaped was Zeus.

ZEUS

Zeus grows up on Crete

In those difficult years, when the reign of Cronus had loosed all manner of evils upon the world, the birth of Zeus seemed like the birth of hope, and his survival like the beginning of a struggle for a better world.

All the deities of Crete hastened to the support of this baby which had first seen the light of day in the cave on Mount Dicte. It was as if something told them that his would be the hands that would free the world from its bonds.

The nymphs and dryads of the woods nurtured the new-born god with particular tenderness. They placed the babe in a golden cradle and rocked it gently to sleep with lulla-bies. And when it woke, they leaned over the cradle and sang it beautiful songs.

There was but one fear: that Cronus might hear the in-fant's wails; and so, whenever it began to cry, some warri-ors, the Curetes, clashed their swords against their shields and made so much noise that they drowned the baby's cries and prevented heartless Cronus from hearing.

The creatures of the forest loved the little god too and helped him in countless ways. Even the bees showed their love for tiny Zeus by bringing him fresh honey every day.

But the animal which rendered the most useful service of all to the young god was the sacred goat, Amaltheia. She loved little Zeus like her own kid, gave him her milk and enveloped him with tender, motherly care, watching over him while he played and never straying from his side.

How Zeus loved Amaltheia! He was never happier than when playing with her and scrambling upon her back, and she, patient and tender-hearted animal that she was, bore patiently with all his games.

One day, however, young Zeus caught hold of one of her horns in play, and such was his strength that the horn came off in his hands. Poor Amaltheia was heart-broken and she gazed at him in reproach. Overcome with remorse at his carelessness, the young god begged her not to grieve and promised her that the horn he had broken off would become the Horn of Plenty and that from it would pour every gift the heart could desire. And that was indeed what happened; every time Amaltheia upturned the horn, piles of luscious fruits would come tumbling from its mouth: figs, grapes, apples and whatever else her appetite fancied.

All the animals of the forest played with Zeus, and the nymphs and dryads offered him beautiful gifts. The nymph Adrasteia gave him a wonderful ball woven from golden rings, and when the young god threw it, it left a shining trail like a shooting star. Little Zeus would go wild with delight playing with this lovely gift.

Zeus takes the great decision

There was also a wise eagle which loved the little god dearly. It would bring him nectar to drink from lands far beyond the ocean and often held him spellbound with tales of the distant places it had visited. Young Zeus listened wide-eyed to the eagle and in the end learned so many things that the nymphs and dryads marvelled at his knowledge.

Zeus grew up handsome, strong and brave. There was none to match him for bravery and knowledge. Then, one day, the eagle spoke to him of Cronus. "You are the son of

Cronus," it told him, "and your father swallowed your brothers for fear that they would take his throne from him."

When fearless Zeus learned of these dreadful deeds, and of how evil and lawlessness still reigned in his father's kingdom, he took a momentous decision: to cast down Cronus from the throne of the gods.

Zeus left Crete immediately, knowing that he must find some course of action. Near a river, he met Oceanus the Titan. The moment the latter set eyes upon the young god, he realized who stood before him and what it was he wanted. "I will help you," he told him, "but first of all you must release your brothers, who are still prisoners inside your father's stomach."

Then he called his daughter Metis, a wise Oceanid who knew every plant which grew upon the earth. He told her that he wanted a potion which would make Cronus disgorge the children he had swallowed. It did not take Metis long to find a suitable herb and to mix the draught that was needed.

Zeus poured the potion into a golden cup and, without revealing who he was, managed to present it to Cronus as choice wine. A single mouthful was enough.

Cronus was immediately seized by violent pains. He could no longer keep down the children in his stomach and began to vomit them up. First came the stone that he had swallowed last, and then, one by one, his five lovely

children. As soon as they emerged, the young gods ran to
embrace the brother who had given them their freedom. By
the time Cronus realised that he had been tricked, it was too
late. Yet matters were not destined to come to such a
speedy end, nor such an easy one.

The Battle of the Titans

Seeing the threat which faced him, Cronus called to his
aid his mighty brothers, the Titans. Zeus, on the other hand,
realised that he could not act until his own brothers were
fully grown.

When at last that time had come, they gathered to unite
their forces in aid of the brother who had freed them. They
were not alone in the daunting struggle that awaited. Other
gods joined them, foremost the mighty Oceanus with his
descendants Cratus, Zelus and Nike who stood for order,
work and peace. These were joined by Prometheus, son of
Iapetus the Titan, a god who loved men deeply. Zeus was
also aided by the one-eyed giants, the Cyclopes, who gave
him thunderbolts to hurl at his enemies. Zeus' final protection was the cloak he wore over his shoulders, made from
the skin of the sacred goat which had suckled him on
Mount Dicte. This magic pelt –the aegis– gave protection
to whoever wore it; and thus, thanks to Amaltheia, Zeus
could not be harmed.

When Cronus saw the preparations made by Zeus, he assembled all the other Titans on Othrys, a mountain strewn with huge rocks which not only gave protection to its defenders, but which they could pluck up with their mighty strength and hurl down on their enemies.

But Zeus and his gods made camp on lofty Olympus. From now on, this was to be their fortress, and later they would build their golden palaces there.

Before the battle started, the gods of Olympus gathered around an altar built by the Cyclopes and swore to fight for a better and a juster world. To achieve that aim, they would willingly give every droplet of their blood and every ounce of their strength until victory was won.

Then they brandished their spears, and uttering a mighty battle cry that made Olympus shake, they charged down upon the Titans. And so began the fearful Battle with the Titans, which was destined to last for ten long years and wreak terrible havoc upon the whole world.

Soon, heavy black clouds had blotted out the sun, the day grew dark and the wind increased to hurricane force, howling like a thousand devils. The clouds scudded across the sky and buffeted against one another as if they, too, were at war. Suddenly, the earth was shaken by Zeus' awesome thunderclaps, and blinding flashes of lightning split the sky asunder. Thunderbolts fell like rain upon the Titans' camp. Then the Titans seized huge rocks and hurled them down with horrifying force on their enemies. Undeterred, the Olympian gods advanced towards Mount Othrys and fell upon the Titans with swords and spears, with flailing arms and gnashing teeth. Like maddened beasts they fought. Such was the hatred between them that no pity was shown on either side in this savage war. The earth was shaken, the forests burst into flame, the sea boiled and the scorching air swirled with black smoke.

The din of battle was terrifying. The boom of thunderclaps came hard upon the hiss of lightning bolts and the clash of weapons mingled with threatening rumbles from underground, whilst the savage cries of the warriors pierced the wild howling of the wind, so loud that they drowned even the most shattering of Zeus' thunderclaps. As the struggle raged, the opposing forces found themselves now on Mount Othrys, now down by the coast, now stretched out across the plain of Thessaly. At one point in the battle, the Titans loosed a cloud of stifling steam upon their enemies and succeeded in driving them back to Mount Olympus. But not for long. Regrouping their forces, the Olympian gods swept down from their mountain again. And so the battle raged to and fro, and earth, sea and sky became one huge hell. Yet neither side could gain the advantage.

At one stage in the battle, Zeus succeeded in freeing the Hundred-handed giants from the depths of the earth where

...Such was the battle with the Titans, th

greatest war the world has ever known...

Cronus had left them lying because he feared their mighty power. Now these mountain-high giants threw themselves into the struggle. The Titans fought back with savage intensity and the earth was so shaken that time and again it split open, revealing the very depths of Tartarus. The destruction reached its climax, however, when Titans, Giants and the Olympian gods fought hand to hand. A terrible earthquake tossed everything into confusion. The mountains toppled down into the sea, the sea surged up on the land, the thunderbolts of Zeus split great mountains asunder and the fires burned so high that tongues of flames licked at the sun itself. The battle was so terrible that it seemed that earth was tumbling into Tartarus and the heavens were plunging from on high.

For nine whole years this terrible war raged between the Titans and the gods of Olympus. By the tenth year, however, the Titans' power had begun to flag, and then a fearful hunting-down began, on land and over seas. Exhausted and undone, the Titans ran to save themselves from the swelling wrath of their enemies. From the furthest limits of the ocean to every far-flung corner of the earth the gods pursued them, bringing the destruction of war even upon what had as yet remained unharmed.

Finally, the fleeing Titans found themselves once more in Greece. It was from here they had set out, and it was here they were to meet their end. In a final mighty surge, the gods of Olympus threw themselves upon the Titans like an all-destroying hurricane. The Titans fought back like wild beasts at bay. Earth and sky mingled, fire and water locked in struggle, and day and night could no longer be told apart.

And as if this chaos and destruction were not enough, the Hundred-handed giants picked up three hundred rocks as huge as mountains and hurled them in a single volley at the Titans' camp. The world had never known a bombardment such as this. And afterwards, when the trembling of the earth had stopped, a strange silence spread over everything.

The fighting was over. The enemy was beaten.

Such was the Battle with the Titans, the greatest war the world has ever known. And although it may sound like pure fantasy, it seems to point to some fearful catastrophe which really occurred. If, on your travels in Greece, you should come across mountains split asunder and others tumbled down into the sea, remember that legendary battle. Perhaps the destruction we now know to have been wrought by earthquakes and natural subsidence was the same that inspired the story-tellers of old to create the myth of the Battle of the Titans.

But our story does not end here.

Binding the Titans with heavy chains forged by the Cyclopes, the gods of Olympus cast them into the murky depths of Tartarus. They sealed this horrible prison with massive iron doors, and before them huge giants kept vigil.

And there, for countless ages, the Titans have lain, longing for the light of day.

The victors made their way back to the sunny slopes of Olympus. They were proud of their great victory, but their eyes clouded over when they gazed down upon the earth. It was unrecognisable. Nothing had been left standing in the appalling struggle. The gods would have a hard task to restore the world to its original beauty.

Zeus' struggle against Typhoon

Yet the Olympians had no time to enjoy their victory before they found themselves facing another fearful enemy.

Mother Earth was enraged at Zeus and the other gods for having been so harsh to her children the Titans. And so she coupled with Tartarus and gave birth to a dreadful monster, Typhoon, a huge dragon taller than the loftiest mountain. It had a hundred heads with black-tongued mouths and fire flashed from its eyes. Its wild roars echoed through the mountain gorges like a raging tempest, sometimes sounding like a lion, sometimes like an infuriated bull. Storms, whirlwinds and all-destroying hurricanes followed in its path.

When the gods of Olympus saw this frightful monster

bearing down upon them, many of them fled in terror to Egypt. Zeus, however, threw himself undaunted upon the monster and struck at it remorselessly with a diamond-bladed sickle. Howling with pain, Typhoon took to flight. But Zeus pursued it, and the thunderbolts of the lord of the world once more shook the earth.

Wherever Typhoon passed, it left destruction in its wake. The whirlwinds and the hurricanes left nothing standing. Whole forests were uprooted, rocks tumbled from the heights and the sea waves rose mountain-high and swept away all before their path.

Eventually, Zeus and Typhoon reached Syria. There, the monster turned at bay and a fierce struggle began. During the fight, Typhoon managed to seize Zeus, and entwined him in its snaky coils. Snatching up the diamond sickle, the monster severed the sinews of Zeus' hands and feet and drew them from his body. Powerless now, the mighty god sank to the ground. Straight away, the monster carried him off to a cave in Cilicia and then ran to find a boulder to block the mouth of the cavern. However, while Typhoon was searching for a large enough stone, Zeus' cunning son Hermes came to the aid of his immortal father. He managed to steal back Zeus' sinews, and with great skill and patience threaded them back into his hands and feet. By the time Typhoon realised what had happened, it was too late. Zeus launched a pitiless rain of searing thunderbolts upon the

monster which fled howling, leaving a path of destruction
in its wake as it dragged itself to safety. On reaching the
mountains of Thrace, it turned once more in desperation
and the peaks were dyed scarlet with the blood of its
wounds. And ever since, that mountain range has been
called "Haemos" or "the Bloody Mountains".

Finally, the hunted monster reached Sicily, where Zeus
hurled a hundred thunderbolts upon it and burned up all its
heads in a single stroke. The monster sank to the ground, its
snaky coils wrapped in flames. To make sure of his enemy,
Zeus heaved a whole mountain down upon Typhoon, but
the fire which consumed the monster broke through to the
mountain's peak and formed a volcano. Etna is its name,
and it has burned to this very day. Even from where he lies
buried, Typhoon can still spread terror and destruction.

Zeus returned to Olympus victorious once more. Now,
the enemies of the gods were all defeated and the Olympians could rule the world in peace. But first the shattered
earth had to be made fruitful once more, and the smile of
peace brought back to the lips of men. And so the gods
divided the world among them, to restore order with all
possible speed. Zeus, the mightiest of them all, assumed the
lordship of the skies. Poseidon became ruler of the seas,

and Hades or Pluto, as he was also called, inherited the Kingdom of the Underworld, where the souls of the dead are taken.

The earth, with all its fruits, became the realm of Demeter, while Hera was both queen of the sky and protector of marriage and giver of children to men. Many other gods also lived on Olympus, but over them all was Zeus, ruler of gods and men.

Olympus

High on the peaks of towering Olympus stood the shining courts of the gods, the vanquishers of the Titans. Their palaces were of solid gold, such as the world had never seen, majestic as the majesty of the gods themselves, radiant with light and splendour. At their gates stood three lovely goddesses, the Hours, who kept the clouds away so that blue skies always stretched above their roofs. The sun always shed its golden light upon them and they were never shadowed by any cloud. There, in those light-bathed palaces, it never rained and no wind ever blew. It was neither cold nor hot, but always temperate and calm.

Only when the gods were away did the Hours cast a veil of clouds around the palaces to hide them. Whenever the immortal ones returned, the three goddesses would scatter the clouds and then the bright palaces of the gods would gleam once more in golden splendour.

Far below, clouds covered the earth. There, spring and summer were followed by autumn and harsh winter. There, after joy came sadness. The gods, too, knew moments of bitter sorrow, but among the gods sorrow is short-lived and happiness never slow to return.

It was a beautiful life on Olympus. At their gatherings, the gods ate ambrosia and drank nectar and rejoiced in their eternal youth – for the gods never grow old. The lovely Graces and the Muses entertained them with dances and with songs. Linking hands, they would dance and sing so delightfully that the gods would sit spellbound, enthralled by their light-footed harmony. And whenever the Muses and the Graces finished dancing, they would always address a hymn of praise to the mightiest god of all, the all-powerful Zeus, father of gods and men.

Indeed all the gods looked upon Zeus as their father, for he was the greatest of the gods, and it was he who had led them in their resounding victory over Cronus and the Titans, in the victory over lawlessness and evil.

Zeus sat in glory on his lofty throne. His wife was the lovely Hera, queen of the sky. Sumptuously dressed, and radiant with beauty and majesty she took her seat on a golden throne at his right hand, and all the gods accorded her the respect which she was due. To Zeus' left stood two other goddesses: Eirene, who hated war, and Nike, the winged goddess of victory, who was always at his side in the struggle against evil.

Zeus reigns over the world

From the kingdom of the sky, Zeus looked down upon earth and ruled over all things. He struck at evil, and established order. Pity the fool who dared break the laws laid down by Zeus, for if he once lowered his brows, black clouds would immediately shroud the skies. When anger seized him, his face would become terrible to behold and blinding sparks would flash from his eyes. He had only to lift his hand and claps of thunder and lightning-bolts would split the heavens apart and shake the whole world. Thus Zeus showed his power, punishing those who disturbed the peace and reminding man of the laws of the gods.

But as long as men were law-abiding and worshipped him, Zeus rewarded them with life-giving sunshine and rain to swell the seed, and men enjoyed the fruits of his generosity.

To ensure that the laws were observed and order maintained, all the other gods supported Zeus and hastened to his command.

Themis, the goddess of law, was always to be found at Zeus' side. She received his commands and conveyed them immediately to mortal men. Thus the laws laid down by the

ruler of the world were established upon earth. Another
goddess, Justice, defended the right and hated falsehood.
Whenever she saw an injustice, she would report it immediately to Zeus and he would deliver his verdict. Woe
betide the law-breaker on whom immortal Zeus passed
sentence, for no harsher punishment could ever have been
imposed.

But if an offender repented before it was too late, and
begged forgiveness, then Zeus in his mercy would always
pardon him, and the cruel Furies would cease to torment
him.

Zeus also sent man joys and sorrows. Two great clay jars
stood at the entrance to the courts of Olympus. One con-
tained all that was good, the other, all the evils of the
world. From them, Zeus drew out both good and evil and
sent them to every man on earth. Alas for the mortal to
whom great Zeus sent gifts only from the jar filled with
evils. He was doomed to misfortune and there was no way
he could save himself, for such was the will of the ruler of
the gods. Whoever received gifts only from the jar of good
fortune was a happy man indeed. But such cases were so
rare as to be almost unheard of. Whoever received both
good and evil equally had reason to be satisfied, for the lot
of man is a hard one.

"It is the destiny of man to suffer," declared Almighty
Zeus, "since even the immortal gods know both joy and

...What is written cannot be unwritten...

bitter sorrow."

But if Zeus dealt out joy and suffering, it was his three daughters, the remorseless Fates, who decided on men's final end. Zeus never intervened in their work, for no one has the right to change the laws which govern life. The Fates thus wielded awesome power and were deaf to all entreaty, all prayers and all sacrifices. Whatever the Fates decided, both gods and mortals had to bow to. The first of them, Clotho, spun the thread of every human life and determined how long each would live. When the thread was cut, then that life, too, was ended. The second, Lachesis, drew with closed eyes the lot which was to befall each mortal. Good or bad, that would be his fate.

Nobody could change the fortune chosen for him by the Fates, for the third of these sisters, Atropos, wrote down on a long scroll, in indelible and unchangeable letters, whatever had been decided by the other two. And what was written, not even the Fates themselves could erase.

Such were the Fates: cruel, stern and majestic.

However, apart from the implacable Fates there lived on Olympus a kind and generous goddess who sent men only good gifts. She was the goddess of happiness and plenty, and her name was Fortune. In her hands she held the Horn of Amaltheia – that same horn Zeus had accidentally pulled from the head of the sacred goat while playing with her in his childhood. Now this light-footed goddess roamed the world and showered upon men the rich gifts which poured from the magic horn. But the eyes of Fortune were always bound and so her gifts fell at random, sometimes favouring the just and sometimes the unjust, sometimes the hard-working and sometimes the lazy. Whoever crossed the path of the goddess was a lucky man, for immediately she would upturn the "horn of plenty" and gifts would pour from it in profusion. Yet the lucky are few in number, for it is rare indeed to cross the path of Fortune – and the truly lucky fewer still; for wealth alone is not enough to bring man happiness.

Zeus himself also helped man in many ways. At Dodona he had a sacred oak tree which bore sweet and succulent acorns. Indeed, it is said that these acorns were the first fruit that men ever ate. Whoever sought the advice of Zeus would come to the holy oak; and after they had sacrificed to the god and humbly made their request, a breeze would spring up and a rustling be heard from among the oak tree's leaves. Then the priests would explain the rustling and deliver the oracle of Zeus. Whatever the oracle's advice, it was respected. No man was ever known to seek the counsel of Zeus at Dodona and then reject it.

But of all the places where Zeus was honoured, the most renowned was Olympia. Here stood the most imposing of all the temples to Olympian Zeus.

Every four years all of Greece, although it was divided

into many city-states, would meet in friendship at Olympia to render homage to the god and to take part in the famous Olympic games. Sacred heralds would announce the event with trumpets in every corner of the land. Even if a war was in progress it would stop, and the thoughts of all would turn to victories of another kind in the Olympic stadium. There, lithe youths would compete in running, jumping, discus throwing, wrestling and other events. Their only reward would be a wreath of olive leaves and their only wish, to win, through fair play, glory both for themselves and for the cities which could boast such fine young men as these.

The twelve gods of Olympus

Many gods lived on Olympus, but the greatest of them were twelve in number. Supreme among them all, of course, was bolt-bearing Zeus who wielded the thunder and the lightning, ruled over the heavens and was father of gods and men. Then came majestic Hera, wife of Zeus, a golden diadem upon her brow. She, too, reigned over the skies and was protector of marriage and women. Then followed the other deities: blue-eyed Athena, with her spear and helmet, goddess of wisdom and the fine arts and of just wars; golden-haired Apollo, with his lyre, god of light and music;

earth-shaking Poseidon, with his trident, god of the sea; stern Artemis, with her bow, goddess of moonlit nights, of forests and the hunt; fair Aphrodite, with her winged son Eros, goddess of beauty and of love; the lame Hephaestus with his stick, god of fire and of the crafts; sad Demeter, her brows wreathed with golden corn, goddess of agriculture; fleet-footed Hermes, with his winged sandals, god of commerce and messenger of Zeus; bloodthirsty Ares, armed for battle, the fearsome god of war; and humble Hestia, goddess of the home and of its ever-burning hearth.

With all these deities, and many others, Zeus reigned from Olympus and maintained peace and order throughout the world.

The wonderful myths which tell of the lives and deeds of the twelve gods of Olympus will be the subject of succeeding chapters.

We have spoken of Zeus, but there is yet more to tell. For since he is the mightiest god of all, Zeus is mentioned very frequently in mythology. For that reason, in the myths which are to follow we shall always have something to say about the life and deeds of the ruler of gods and men.

HERA

In the land of the Hesperides

In the days before the rise of Zeus, when the fearsome Titan Cronus ruled over gods and men, a goddess sat upon a rock, holding a little girl in her arms. The name of this goddess was Rhea, and she was Cronus' wife. Her face was sad and her expression thoughtful — and with good reason: She wished to save her children from her husband, whose one desire was to destroy them all lest they topple him from his throne. Now she held her little daughter Hera in her arms and racked her brains trying to think of a place where she could hide her.

It was the hour when the sun sinks towards its rest, and a breathtaking view spread itself before her. As she gazed out upon the magnificent sunset a thought suddenly crossed her mind. She remembered that beneath those parti-coloured clouds lay the fairest land in all the world, the land of the Hesperides. There lived her three sisters, the Hours, and now the time had come when she had need of them.

The land of the Hesperides lay far away, its shores beyond the reach of man; and it was not until much later that it was visited by the mythical heroes Heracles and Perseus. Above all, Cronus' affairs never carried him so far afield; he had never visited the land of the Hesperides.

"That is where I shall hide my daughter," Rhea cried, and swift as the wind she set out for the distant, brightly-coloured West.

The journey to that earthly paradise was enchanting; the further west she journeyed, the more beautiful everything around her became. Sky, earth, and sea were all bathed in countless colours, and when she stepped down into the land of the Hesperides, its radiance seemed to enfold her like an aura, holding her momentarily spellbound. Happy indeed are the Hesperides, the goddesses who live and rule in that place. Happy, too, are the three sisters, the Hours, who also live there, far from the tyranny of Cronus.

The Hours came happily forward to meet their sister, but as they drew nearer their faces fell at the sight of Rhea's troubled and anxious expression. She laid the child gently at their feet and then, sobbing, embraced them one by one.

"Unhappy mother that I am," she cried. "For years now I have been losing my children. Their own father swallows them for fear that they will one day cast him from his throne, just as he overthrew his own father, the once-great Uranus. Thanks to Zeus, I now see them again, for he forced Cronus to bring them forth into the light once more, but alas! I fear that I must lose them yet again. Cronus is in real danger now, and who knows what schemes he may be plotting to do away with them for a second time? And so, kind sisters, I am now bringing you my daughter, Hera. A prophecy foretells that she will become foremost among goddesses, revered by mortals and immortals alike. Here, in this faraway land, Cronus will never come to do her harm."

The Hours received little Hera gladly, and Rhea, her fears now laid to rest, set out once more for Greece.

The Hours brought Hera up with all the loving care of true mothers. They joined in her games, and taught her countless things about the gods, nature and the world.

Hera grew into a girl so beautiful that the birds and the beasts of the forest were dazzled when she passed. Yet her beauty did not turn her head. She was fond of study and learning, and wished to become a goddess worthy and capable of aiding both gods and mortals; and so she asked the Hours ceaseless questions on every subject under the sun. These fond foster-mothers took her for walks, showed her the sky and the earth, and explained how the winter

comes, and the spring, and then the summer. They would
often take her to a mountain, show her the clouds and the
sea and explain how thunder and lightning and storms are
caused. When night fell, they would show her the starry
sky and teach her to pick out the constellations. Hera never
tired of listening to all the Hours had to tell. She had now
learned all the mysteries of the skies and felt immortal
power stirring within her. She loved the sky, and would
exclaim with girlish simplicity: "Oh, how I would love to
be Queen of the Heavens!"

Iris, one of the goddesses of the sky, was very fond of
the lovely Hera. Often, to please her, she would deck the
heavens with the delicate hues of the rainbow, and Hera
could never gaze deeply enough upon its beauty. Of all the
creatures that lived in the lovely land of the Hesperides,
Hera was especially fond of a large bird whose tail resembled a starry sky. This was the peacock, which became
Hera's inseparable companion.

Hera and Zeus

One day, Hera was sitting alone on the edge of a rock by
the sea. The Hours had schooled her in the art of control-
ling the weather, and she now wished to put her powers to
the test. She made a gentle movement with her hand, a
gesture which resembled a timid command – and lo! black

clouds filled the sky, the calm of the day was shattered by bursts of thunder and lightning shafts, and life-giving rain watered the earth. Hera was happy in the knowledge that she was now a goddess of mighty power, and her face became radiant with beauty.

At that moment an eagle appeared, winging its way toward her. On its back sat a handsome youth. This was Zeus, the god who would one day rule the heavens and the earth.

Climbing from the eagle's back, he approached Hera and said: "Is it you, beautiful goddess, who gives orders to the skies?"

"Yes, it is I," replied the young goddess humbly. "It is an art taught me by the Hours. I love the sky and my dream is to become..."

"To become Queen of the Sky," said Zeus, who had read her thoughts. "Climb with me upon the eagle and I shall take you to Greece, and, if you wish, you shall become my wife."

Hera needed no second asking. She had already decided to become Zeus' faithful and devoted companion. She knew that it was to him she owed her freedom and she knew his brave heart; so she joyfully took her place beside him upon the eagle.

Soon they were waving farewell to the Hours from on high. The goddesses had seen all that passed between them, and now, with tears in their eyes, they wished all happiness to their beloved Hera and her companion.

The eagle swooped in a great circle over the Hesperides in a last farewell to the land which had raised Hera to womanhood, and then smoothly but swiftly set wing for Greece.

Seated happily at Zeus' side, Hera had scarcely time to realize it before they were over the land of the Hellenes. And now she gazed down as if entranced upon the country which had given her birth. She looked in awe upon Olympus, was delighted by the sight of Mount Ida, and caught her first glimpse of Argos, Mycenae and Samos. It was enchanting, this land of her great father Cronus.

But then Zeus reminded Hera of Cronus' harshness and of how he had swallowed both her and her brothers.

"With the help of Oceanus the Titan and his daughter I was able to set you free," he added. He went on to explain how wicked and lawless was the rule of Cronus and how it was that so much evil had fallen upon the world.

"It is both our duty and our destiny to cast out Cronus and the Titans from the throne of the gods, so that order and justice may reign upon the earth."

Hera listened to Zeus in astonishment. His words rang so true in her ears that she was determined to offer him whatever help he might ask of her. In the difficult years which followed, the years of the fearful war against Cronus and the Titans, Hera stood firm at Zeus' side, fighting as his equal and giving to the limit of her powers without ever counting the cost.

When victory finally came, she saw that Zeus was now the all-powerful ruler of gods and men, and her heart swelled with joy. Soon she would be wedded to the lord of the skies and Olympus; and as his wife, she, too, would hold sway over the heavens. Her childhood dream would soon become reality.

On Olympus, preparations were made for a wedding splendid beyond belief. The Graces decked Hera in a robe woven from threads of gold; they adorned her with price-less earrings, necklaces and bracelets, and on her silken hair they placed a royal diadem, whilst Iris brought a train delicate as spiders' webs and shimmering with all the colours of the rainbow. Thus bedecked, Hera shone radiant among the immortals with all the beauty and freshness of youth, a worthy queen for Olympus.

Hera sat at Zeus' side in majesty, upon a tall golden throne, whilst all the gods brought precious gifts and laid them at their feet.

Suddenly, a magnificent tree bearing golden apples sprang up inside the very palace. The gods looked on in astonishment, dazzled by its beauty and its splendour. However, they soon realized that this was a gift of the goddess Earth for the wedding of Hera and Zeus.

To please Hera, the Hours brought the most beautiful spring day, and a light, cool breeze wafted the fragrance of flowers among the courts of Olympus.

In her happiness, Hera felt herself wrapped in the sweet strains of a heavenly melody. In her ears there echoed the music of gods. It was the Muses and the Graces and all the immortals of Olympus joining their voices in praise of the mighty couple. It was Apollo with his lyre, Hermes with his flute, and winged cherubs with their pipes and horns: a torrent of sound of incomparable beauty.

Soon the melody was taken up by other voices beyond the bounds of Olympus. It was sung by the dryads in the forests and by the nymphs and oceanides on river bank and sea shore. Now the music of the gods re-echoed to the furthest reaches of the earth. Zeus and Hera came out of the palace and listened in wonder. The other gods followed them enthralled. They walked forth upon clouds of many colours, forming a heavenly procession which moved onwards over mountains and seas. All nature, robed in the fresh tints of spring, sang the praises of Queen Hera and almighty Zeus.

Glowing with beauty, Hera walked proudly at her husband's side, rejoicing in these moments that were to make her the first lady of the world. In her happiness, she felt that she must do all in her power to help a world that so rejoiced in her own joy.

Helone drags her feet

However, although the gods and all nature rejoiced at this sacred wedding, there was one foolish nymph who did not wish to go to the great feast. Her name was Helone, and she pretended that she could not walk. She dragged her way slowly along the road, for she had no intention of reaching Olympus. The wedding was already over and she was still far away, feigning painful haste, though she was really walking as slowly as she could go.

When Hera learned of this, she was so angry that, despite the happiness of the great day, she could not let Helone go unpunished. She turned her into an animal encased in a hard shell, so she would never again be able to walk faster than she had done when going to the wedding. This animal is the familiar tortoise of our days, or "helone" as the Greeks call it.

The wanderings of Io

Now Hera ruled on Olympus, and, like Zeus, wielded the golden sceptre. She would drive forth from the courts of Olympus seated upon a golden chariot, pulled through the heavens by two magnificent horses. With Zeus, she ruled over the sky and the clouds, over rain, thunderbolts and storms.

As in the sky, so Hera wielded great power upon earth. First among goddesses, she was first, too, among mortals and the protector of all women.

She was present at every wedding; a perfect example of the faithful and devoted wife, she wanted every human wife to show a like devotion to her husband and raise a happy family. For this reason she never forgave any woman who failed to keep her vows — but any woman who came between her and Zeus she punished a hundred times more harshly.

And so, when Io, a beautiful princess of Argos, attracted the attentions of her lord, the anger of Hera was terrible to behold.

In this case, Io was not really to blame. For was not Zeus all-powerful, and could any mortal resist him? He always did whatever he wanted without taking anyone into consideration, not even his own devoted wife.

Hera suffered more than words can tell on account of this, but she could not set her face against the ruler of the world. And now that Zeus wanted Io, Hera's anger turned against the unlucky princess.

The torments Io suffered as a result of Hera's rage were terrible indeed.

Knowing what lay in store for Io, Zeus himself tried to

...The melody he played was a lullaby so sweet and smooth
that even the watchful Argus could not resist its spell...

protect her, changing her into a white heifer so that Hera
would be unable to find her. But even that was in vain. As
soon as Hera saw the snow-white animal, she realized by
its beauty that it must be Io and craftily asked Zeus to give
her the lovely beast as a gift. Zeus was unable to deny his
wife this favour and gave it to her. Once the unfortunate
creature had fallen into her hands, Hera led it to the top of a
hill, tied it to a tree and left it there guarded by the fearsome Argus, a giant with a hundred eyes. There seemed to
be no way of escaping him, for even when he slept, fifty of
his eyes remained open and looked around threateningly.
Caught in this hopeless situation, poor Io suffered agonies
and looked despairingly towards the heavens, as if seeking
help. Zeus saw how desperately unhappy she was and took
pity on her. So he called for quick-thinking Hermes and
ordered him to do whatever he could to set her free.

Hermes swiftly reached the spot where Io stood guarded
by Argus. Pretending to pay no attention to the heifer, he
got into conversation with the giant and behaved in a
friendly manner towards him. Then, as if to please Argus,
he took out his flute and began to play. But the melody he
played was a lullaby so sweet and smooth that even the
watchful Argus could not resist its spell, and fell into a
sleep so deep that all his hundred eyes closed, one by one.
Thus Hermes managed to set Io free.

If only the princess' sufferings had ended here! But

when Hera learnt that the white heifer had been released, she sent a terrible horsefly in its pursuit, a fly as big as a bat with a venomous sting which caused unbearable pain. The shock of the first sting hurled Io into the air and she took to her heels to escape it; but the horsefly pursued her relentlessly, stinging with all its poisonous power. Maddened by the pain, Io fled as fast as her legs would carry her, but the horsefly winged in upon her again and again and drove its poisonous dart into her flesh. The unhappy Io was pursued from coast to coast. Believing that safety might lie among the waves she jumped into the sea – and ever since then we have called these waters the Ionian Sea. But even there the horsefly pursued its prey, so Io came ashore once more and ran bellowing off in the direction of Thrace. From there she ran northwards, passed through the land of the Scythians, and finally reached the Caucasus, where Prometheus the Titan, the great soothsayer, lay bound in chains and nailed to a rock by order of Zeus.

Flecked with foam and dripping blood from a hundred open wounds, Io was a very different sight from the lovely princess of Argos she had once been. She stood before the chained Titan and with pleading eyes begged him:

"Great Prometheus, you who know the fates of gods and men, forget your own tortures for a moment and tell me when and where my sufferings will end!"

"In Egypt," Prometheus replied, "where the great Nile

pours into the sea. It will take you a long time to reach
there; your wanderings will seem endless, and you will
have bitter sufferings to endure before you reach your goal;
but there you will find salvation and become a woman
again."

When Prometheus had uttered these words he gave a
great cry of pain, for an eagle sent by Zeus had come, as it
did each day, and thrust its beak into the entrails of the
chained Titan.

Poor Io fled like a maddened beast, pursued once more
by the monster horsefly. She passed over the snowy Caucasus and, running wildly, reached the land of the Amazons,
which has been called Ionia ever since. Then she crossed a
sea filled with Gorgons who had writhing tangles of poisonous snakes in place of hair. She managed to reach the
further shore and escape from the clutches of the Gorgons,
but then she found herself in a land whose skies were thick
with one-eyed vultures. They smelt the blood from her
open wounds and swooped down upon her, tearing her
pitilessly with their cruel beaks. In her efforts to escape
them she became lost in a huge desert where she could not
find a single drop of water to cool her parched lips. And
still the terrible horsefly pursued her, and still it stabbed its
venom into her flesh. Finally, after many more wanderings,
Io reached the mountains of Ethiopia and found the source
of the Nile. Taking courage at the sight, she began a last,

long, mad gallop northwards. This was the final stretch on the long road of her sufferings, but even so the horsefly did not leave her for an instant. At last she reached Egypt; and there, on the banks of the Nile, she saw Zeus himself standing before her. Io's sufferings had come to an end. Zeus immediately killed the horsefly and then laid his hand upon Io's head. By that simple contact Io became a beautiful princess once more. Zeus did not stay a moment longer. He returned to Olympus; but through the mere touch of his hand Io gave birth to a son whom she called Epaphus, which means "touch". This child became the first king of Egypt and forefather of a long line of heroes. From this line sprang Heracles, the greatest hero of all Greece.

The ingratitude of Ixion

It was Hera's constant wish that, by her conduct, she would show both gods and men what a good and serious wife should be. Her dignity and devotion to Zeus were known to all, and for this reason everybody treated her with great respect – all, that is, except one who tried to make her his own. His name was Ixion.

Ixion was a cruel king in the land of the Lapiths. He committed so many misdeeds that both gods and men combined to drive him out of his country. Ixion fled, but nowhere could he find shelter. As soon as he came across mortals they would drive him away with stones and clubs, and whenever he sat down to regain his breath in some deserted spot, a god would appear and cast him out. There was not a soul would take pity on cruel Ixion. Finally, he found his way to a temple of Zeus. His clothes were torn and he was bloody and dirty – a far cry from the once great and fearsome ruler of the Lapiths. Knowing how readily Zeus offered hospitality, Ixion entered the temple without fear. As soon as he was inside, he fell exhausted upon the floor, but once he had recovered a little he raised himself upon his knees and holding his arms aloft cried out:

"O Zeus, protector of all strangers, lord and beggar alike, receive me, too, for I humbly beg your forgiveness."

It was indeed true that the mighty Zeus would never refuse a stranger hospitality, and when he saw the sorry state into which the once-great Ixion had fallen, he pitied him as he had never pitied anyone before. To save him from the wrath of gods and men, he made the greatest gesture of hospitality that was in his power: he brought Ixion to Olympus and sat him at the table of the gods, at Hera's very side. Ixion ate ambrosia and drank the nectar of the gods and thus became, like them, immortal. But even this was not enough for him, it seems: now he wanted Zeus' wife for himself. Hera tried to make him understand that she was a goddess who held marriages together, not one who broke their sacred bond, but Ixion had no intention of

...And since that day Ixion has spun snake-bound in the
flames, forever crying: Hospitality is sacred!...

respecting her wishes. As for his own desires, his conduct made them plain to everyone on Olympus.

Zeus could scarcely believe that this was how his hospitality was repaid. Curious to learn the extent of Ixion's ingratitude, he transformed a cloud, Nephele, into the shape of Hera. Thinking that Nephele was Hera herself, Ixion made her his own, and she even gave birth to a child. The result of the union between Ixion and Nephele was as monstrous as the union itself – a creature half man and half horse called a centaur. After having showered such hospitality upon Ixion, Zeus could hardly let his ingratitude go unpunished; so he called for Hermes and ordered him to catch Ixion and tie him with snakes to a wheel and to place fire beneath it.

And since that day the immortal Ixion has spun snakebound in the flames, forever crying: "Hospitality is sacred!"

This is how Zeus punished Ixion, who broke a holy rule: never do harm to a person who offers you a kindness.

Hebe, the cupbearer of the gods

Hera and Zeus had two sons, Hephaestus and Ares. They also had a daughter, whom they called Hebe, which means "youth". Hebe was everything a good daughter should be: she would make ready her mother's chariot and horses and wash the clothes of her brother Ares, but her favourite task was to offer ambrosia and nectar to the gods in golden bowls and chalices.

Ambrosia was the food of immortality which prevented the gods from ever becoming old. Hebe delighted in serving it, for by this deed she offered the gods eternal youth and did justice to her name.

Hebe was loved by everyone on Olympus, above all by her parents; and later, when Heracles became immortal, they married her to that renowned hero.

After her marriage, she continued to be a support to her parents, and to her mother in particular. At the festivals held by mortals to honour Hera, Hebe was always to be found at her side. For this reason, she would often go to Argos, for there stood the most splendid of all the temples in her mother's name. But her favourite temple was the Heraion at Olympia. There, girls would compete in races in honour of Hera, and whoever came first would be crowned with a wreath of olive leaves and be honoured above all other girls in Greece.

APHRODITE

The birth of Aphrodite

One spring morning long ago, in distant Cyprus, the nymphs and dryads of the forest awoke with a feeling of surprise. This morning was different: It was cooler and more fragrant; the light was clearer and the earth greener; the sky was bluer and the flowers more thickly-strewn and beautiful; the birds and the beasts seemed happier. What could be happening?

The mystery was soon solved: a new goddess had sprung from the waves and set foot upon the island. She was the goddess of beauty and love, the daughter of Uranus, the peerlessly lovely Aphrodite.

How had all this come about?

When Uranus, then lord of gods and men, was wounded with a sickle by the treacherous Cronus and lost his throne, a small piece of his flesh fell into the sea off the island of Kythira. On the spot where it had dropped, a small patch of foam formed. It grew and grew until suddenly, from the midst of the snow-white mass, a girl sprang. This was Aphrodite, the daughter of Uranus and the foam and the fairest creature, mortal or immortal, ever to appear upon this earth.

At the sight of the lovely goddess the sea swelled with joy and the fish jumped into the foam to delight her. Sea-birds brought a great shell like a chariot and the goddess seated herself upon it. With a fluttering of countless wings and harsh shrieks of joy the gulls drew the sea-borne chariot across the waves to Cyprus.

When the goddess set foot upon the island all nature rejoiced. As she passed by, fragrant flowers of many hues sprang up and a carpet of cool green appeared beneath her feet, whilst overhead the birds sang cheerfully.

The Hours and the Graces came at once to welcome and to tend her. They dressed the lovely goddess in a shining robe, they combed her golden hair until it was even more beautiful than before, and on her brow they placed a golden diadem decked with fragrant violets. They fastened sparkling earrings upon her ears and adorned her neck with their own golden necklaces, whilst her lovely hands they decorated with glittering rings and bracelets.

And thus the fairest girl and goddess ever born was adorned with the world's most beautiful jewels, and by the hands most worthy to perform that task.

The radiance of her loveliness transformed the world. Now the sun shone brighter and the birds sang more sweetly. The wild creatures of the forest would await her passing and gambol joyfully around her. Aphrodite walked proudly through a rejoicing nature, exulting in the power bestowed upon her by her grace and beauty. As yet, the other gods had not set eyes upon her, but soon the Hours and the Graces set the lovely girl upon a billowy cloud and carried her swiftly to Olympus.

So great was the impression her beauty made upon the Olympians that it seemed as if blindness had dimmed their eyes. They soon realised who she was and hastened to embrace her. The charm of the goddess of beauty was irresistible. Everybody wanted to talk with her and enjoy her delightful company. And she would reply gracefully, her queenly face glowing with happiness, and her sweet words now accompanied by a charming smile, now by a captivating gesture, and now by a look which held her listener enthralled.

Aphrodite was queen of eternal beauty and goddess of love, and from the towering heights of Olympus she ruled over the hearts of men.

Helped by her little son, winged Eros, who was armed with a bow whose arrows never missed their mark, she dealt men both sorrow and joy, happiness and bitter disappointments. The gods, too, were often smitten by Aphrodite's shafts, for there was no one, mortal or immortal, who could resist the power of the Cyprian goddess, as she is sometimes called.

Aphrodite protected all those who know the meaning of true love, and of all living creatures, she loved doves best, for these birds couple as soon as they are born, and their love endures until death.

Ctesylla and Ermohares

One of Aphrodite's duties as goddess of love was to protect marriage and to see that wedding vows were kept. Nothing enraged her more than a broken promise, and woe betide the man who did not keep his word. Alcidamus was harshly punished for such a fault, and this is how the story goes:

At a religious festival, a young Athenian named Ermohares set eyes upon the daughter of Alcidamus, Ctesylla, and fell in love with her at first sight. He took an apple, which is a symbol of great love, carved a few words upon it and threw it to Ctesylla.

The beautiful girl picked up the apple and, as was the

custom, read out aloud the phrase which was written upon it. The young man swore to the goddess Aphrodite that he would take Ctesylla for his wife.

However, Ctesylla was shamed by Ermohares' gesture. She threw the apple back and hurriedly left the feast. But the young man, deeply in love, went to the girl's father and asked for her hand in marriage. Alcidamus saw that he was a good young man with serious intentions so he gave his consent. The young man went happily home and told his parents, who were as overjoyed as he was.

But the happiest of all was Ctesylla herself, for she realised that Ermohares was an honest and reliable young man who deserved all the love she could give him.

However, matters did not proceed as happily as they had begun. Shortly afterwards, Alcidamus broke off his daughter's engagement without consulting anyone, because a young man from a wealthy family had come to ask for her hand.

When Ermohares learned of this, he ran to find his beloved Ctesylla. But he could find her nowhere. He searched the whole town and then combed the surrounding forest and finally, when dusk fell, went into a temple, exhausted. And whom did he find in the temple but Ctesylla! In despair over her father's cruel decision, she had gone there to seek the help of the gods.

"Ctesylla!" She had hardly heard him call her name before they were in each other's arms, their eyes misty with tears.

Ctesylla realised that her love for Ermohares was so great that she could not live without him. So, with the blessing of the goddess Aphrodite, she swore to become his faithful companion her whole life long.

Now no other way was open to her but to flee her father's home in secret. She told her nurse of her troubles and the old woman, who loved her like a daughter, agreed to be of assistance. And so, one night, Ctesylla ran away from her father's house and the next day she married Ermohares.

Blind with rage, Alcidamus smashed everything that lay within his reach and shouted that he would kill them both. He scoured the countryside in search of them, but all in vain.

Some time later, however, news came to him that his daughter had given birth to her first child.

This happy event softened the heart of Alcidamus. Feelings of fatherly love welled up inside him and he was overcome with happiness. Now he could hardly wait to see his daughter and his little grandchild.

But his joy was short-lived, for grave misdeeds are often followed by grave consequences. And now a second message came to tell Alcidamus of his daughter's death.

For Alcidamus had sworn on the sacred laurel that he would give his daughter to Ermohares, and because he broke his vow he was punished by Ctesylla's death.

Yet Aphrodite pitied the young mother who had been made to pay so high a price for her father's broken promises.

As they were carrying Ctesylla to her grave, a white bird came winging out of her coffin. When they opened it, they found it empty; the goddess Aphrodite had transformed Ctesylla into a dove.

And every night, above Ctesylla's home, as Ermohares lay sleeping with his child, a white dove fluttered in the darkness.

Pygmalion creates Galatea

Yet if Aphrodite punished those who did not obey the laws of the gods, she never failed to reward those who showed proper respect. She heard their pleas and made them happy. Here is one such story.

There was a great sculptor in Cyprus whose name was Pygmalion. He wished to marry and raise a family, but he could not find the woman he wanted. Pygmalion's fame, not only as a talented artist, but as a wealthy and handsome young man, had spread far beyond the boundaries of Cyprus and Greece, and renowned matchmakers brought him women from every corner of the world. They presented lovely Cypriot girls to him, rich Athenian ladies, princesses from Mycenae, delightful maidens from Sicily and Crete. Others brought him lovely, golden-garbed creatures from Carthage, Egypt and Babylon, and even from places far further afield such as Scythia – and from the land of the Hesperides itself, so some say. None of them pleased Pygmalion, for he was seeking a beauty that lay in simplicity and virtue.

Having finally lost all hope of finding the woman he wished for, Pygmalion shut himself in his workshop and set to work. He took a snow-white block of marble and began to carve a statue of the woman of his dreams, an image of the maiden he was seeking.

Pygmalion created a figure so lovely that its face, its stance and its whole being told one that here indeed was the beauty that lay in simplicity and virtue.

The great sculptor worked with such passion and artistry that it seemed as if at any moment the lovely maiden would move and speak.

Pygmalion loved his statue so fervently that he would no longer do anything but gaze at it in admiration and find endless ways of enhancing the beauty and perfection of his work.

"I wanted a wife like this," he would say again and again, "but it seems that there is no such woman in the whole world."

The time came round for the feast of the goddess

Aphrodite, and Pygmalion took a white heifer and went to offer it to the goddess.

When he arrived before the altar he said: "O great Aphrodite, goddess of beauty and love, you who can do what no mortal can, send me a maiden of the kind I long for, like the one I carved in my workshop."

At that very instant a flame shot up from the altar fire and Pygmalion knew the goddess had heard his plea.

He made his way happily homewards – and when he arrived, what a sight awaited him!

He found the whole house spotless, a fire burning in the hearth and food simmering in a cauldron. He went straight to the room where the statue stood, and to his astonished delight saw it walk and heard it speak to him: "Pygmalion, I am the goddess' gift to you. I am your wife."

Then Pygmalion took in his arms the woman of his own creation. She was warm, soft, lovely and overflowing with tenderness. And since her skin was as white as milk, he named her Galatea, from the Greek word for milk.

Pygmalion and Galatea were later blessed with a daughter whom they called Paphos – and the town of Paphos on Cyprus has borne her name to this very day.

Narcissus and Echo

Yet, whatever good will Aphrodite may have shown

towards those that honoured her, she was relentlessly
severe with those who did not respect her and dared to
scorn her powers. The handsome Narcissus suffered harsh
punishment for treating her like this.

Narcissus was a youth so dazzled by his own beauty that
he thought his equal was not to be found in the whole wide
world. Among gods and men alike, he was the only one in
whose heart the arrows of Aphrodite's son could not find
their mark and make it throb with love. Narcissus knew this
and gloried in it, and treated the goddess with disdain. He
believed he had no need of her, and for a very simple
reason: Narcissus' admiration was reserved for himself and
for nothing and nobody else.

And yet the day came when Aphrodite's bolt pierced
Narcissus to the heartstrings. But let us begin the tale from
the beginning.

Narcissus, the son of the sacred river Cephissus, was so
handsome that when he went walking in the forest, as he
liked to do, he would flutter the heart of every nymph and
dryad that happened to cross his path. Narcissus would
swell with pride at the impression he created. He never fell
in love himself, of course; he merely wanted others to fall
in love with him. And at each new conquest he would glow
with self-esteem. Such were his feelings when he saw that
the nymph Echo had fallen in love with him, and he
brushed her aside in a manner at once cruel and self-

satisfied.

Lovely though she was, Echo lacked the power of speech and could only repeat the last syllables of what she heard.

She first set eyes on Narcissus as he was taking one of his usual walks through the forest, pausing at every other step to admire the spring in his pace and the splendid way he held his body.

Echo had never seen such a proud and handsome youth. She was ashamed to meet his gaze, however, and quickly hid behind a bush.

Narcissus, who had seen her out the corner of his eyes, shouted out in an abrupt tone of voice:

"Who is hiding in the place where I am?"

"...I am," came back the nymph's frightened voice.

"Where are you?" asked the young man, his voice softening. "Come here!"

"...Here!" came the nymph's voice again.

But Narcissus could see nothing.

"Come out," he cried. "I want to see you!"

"...To see you!" repeated the same voice, delighted now; and with these words Echo appeared, radiant with beauty, and ran towards the young man.

But neither her beauty nor the love for him that shone in her eyes could touch Narcissus' heart. The evidence of his conquest was reward enough for him.

"Get out of here!" he shouted. "Do you think that I am for the likes of you, you fool?"

"...Fool!" repeated Echo, and ran away crying with shame and disappointment.

Now, as goddess of love, Aphrodite could not let Narcissus go unpunished. Here is how she made him pay for his heartlessness:

While Narcissus was walking in the forest soon after, he felt thirsty and wanted to drink some water. After searching for a while, he found a small pool. Its crystal-clear waters were so well protected from the wind, and the spot was so peaceful, that everything around its banks was reflected as if in a mirror.

As he bent to drink, Narcissus saw his own face in the water. At that moment, Eros fired a dart that struck him to the heart.

Not knowing that the face mirrored in the water was his own, Narcissus was overwhelmed with love for what he saw. Never in all his life had he set eyes on such a handsome face. Eros had followed his mother's instructions well: the youth who had never known the meaning of love was now desperately infatuated with his own image.

Narcissus gazed into the pool as if he could never be satisfied. After a while he reached down towards the figure in the water, and saw that it made the same gesture. Then he bent to kiss it, but, as soon as his lips touched the sur-

...Never in all his life had he set eyes on such a
handsome face...

face, the image shattered. Soon the ripples subsided, the handsome face appeared again, and once more he lowered his head in rapture to offer it a kiss. Again the same thing happened. Time after time Narcissus was frustrated, until at last he was plunged into despair. He refused to leave the lakeside, but knelt there without eating or drinking, thinking only of the figure in its waters. Whole days and nights went by, and still Narcissus had not moved. He was becoming weaker hour by hour, but the thought of abandoning that unattainable face did not even cross his mind.

Finally, however, as he sat there gazing at the reflection, he realised whose it was and cried out in despair: "Alas! The figure I see in the water is my own, and I shall never be able to touch it!"

But even now that he had learned the truth he could not bring himself to leave, for the image held him even deeper in its thrall.

And so Narcissus stayed by the pool, without eating, without drinking, and without thinking of anything but his own reflection. And there by the lakeside he died, his pale face mirrored in the quiet waters.

Such was the punishment of the handsome Narcissus, whose fate was to never love anyone but himself.

All the nymphs and dryads of the forest wept for the splendid youth, and Echo most of all. She sat by his side and cried until night fell and sleep overcame her. When she awoke, Narcissus was no more. In his place grew a fragrant flower. We call it "narcissus" and it is the flower of death.

Grief-stricken, Echo wandered through the forest until she died of her sorrow. But her voice remained, and if you go into woods and shout loudly, you will be able to hear it. It will always answer with your last word.

Aphrodite and Adonis

But now the time had come for Aphrodite herself to taste the bitterness of death. Just as Echo had lost Narcissus, so the goddess of love lost her darling Adonis.

Adonis, son of Cyniras, king of Cyprus, was born one spring in the forest from the trunk of a myrtle which suddenly split open and brought him forth into the world. It is said that this myrtle was really Smyrna, queen of Cyprus, whom the gods had transformed into a tree in punishment for some evil deed.

Adonis grew up in the forest, tended by the nymphs, and became the most handsome young man the world had ever seen. Indeed, there were many who felt that he surpassed even the golden-haired Apollo in beauty.

So divine were Adonis' looks that two goddesses quarrelled over which of them would take him for her own. One of these was Aphrodite, and the other Persephone. Finally it was Aphrodite who won and now she and Adonis ran together through the forest, playing happily beneath the golden shafts of sunlight.

There are many who know the meaning of true love, but none can be compared with the goddess of love herself. For the sake of Adonis she gave up the airy halls of Olympus and hastened to Cyprus to be with her beloved. Neither cold nor heat nor storm could keep Aphrodite from his side.

Adonis was fond of hunting and Aphrodite would often go with him in chase of deer and hares and wild goats. But she warned him not to hunt bears, wild boar or wolves, for fear that he might come to some harm.

One day, however, when Aphrodite was away, Adonis spied a huge wild boar. The goddess' warnings did not even cross his mind. He approached it on silent steps and prepared himself to strike.

Alas! At the very moment he was taking aim, the boar suddenly threw itself upon him and impaled him on its savage tusks.

Aphrodite sensed that some misfortune had befallen her beloved Adonis, and hastened in search of him. She combed the forest, and in her haste and anxiety her sandals slipped from her feet, which soon became scratched and bleeding. When she finally found Adonis, he was already breathing his last.

Beside herself with grief, she collapsed upon his dead body. The heart of the goddess of love was torn asunder by unbearable pangs of sorrow.

Alone and desolate, she wandered through the forest weeping over the cruel loss of her beloved. Her tears watered the earth, and where they fell anemones sprang up. From the drops of blood which trickled from her feet, the roses, which till then had all been white, were dyed a crimson hue.

Aphrodite's pain and grief over the loss of the noble youth awoke the sympathy of every god on Olympus; and the mighty Zeus, ruler of gods and men, pitied her most of all. And so he commanded his brother Hades to allow Adonis to return to earth for six months every year.

The command was obeyed. Every year, Adonis returns to earth and, in a remote forest on Cyprus, is received with tears of joy by the goddess who adored him. Then all nature rejoices with her and puts on its brightest clothes. The birds sing in celebration of the return of Adonis to his beloved and the coming of spring to the earth. But when the time comes for Adonis to return to the underworld, Aphrodite gives him a last, heartbroken kiss and the whole world mourns. The sky becomes dark with clouds because Adonis has gone, and because autumn is coming and the harsh winter.

But Adonis will come again, and with him will come the spring with its blossom and its joys. The happy festivals of April will return, too, when men praise Adonis, Aphrodite and the blossoming spring, while, somewhere in the forest, the divine couple run and play and laugh in shared delight.

APOLLO

The birth of Apollo

The sacred island of Delos was not always fixed in its present position in the archipelago of the Cyclades, but drifted endlessly over seas and oceans – until one day a goddess set foot upon its shores, fear and anguish written upon her face. Her name was Leto. In her womb she bore two of Zeus' children, Apollo and Artemis, and now she was seeking a place where she could give birth.

"O island," cried the goddess, "age-long wanderer upon the waves, give me refuge and let me bear my children on your soil. I have been hunted all over the world by the

Python, the fearsome monster which jealous Hera sent after me to seek revenge. I have been to Attica and to Thrace, to Lesbos, Chios – everywhere. Nowhere will they let me give birth. They all fear the terrible Python and the wrath of Hera. Receive me now, o island, you who know what endless wandering means, and I promise you that Apollo, the son whom I shall bear, will raise on your soil a splendid temple that will make your name renowned."

Hardly had these words passed Leto's lips when a violent trembling shook the whole of Delos. Two huge rocks thrust themselves upwards from the sea bed and the island settled firmly upon them, fixing itself once and for all in the position where it lies today. Thus Delos received Leto.

Immediately, a host of other goddesses came to Leto's aid. Nine whole days and nights she was in labour and when, on the tenth night, she finally bore her children, the darkness immediately turned to bright daylight and the sun appeared in majesty in the heavens, casting its golden beams upon the isle. Truly, it could not have been otherwise, for the son that she bore was the god of light, golden-haired Apollo; and with him was born stern Artemis, goddess of moonlit nights.

Four days passed and already Apollo was a lithe youth filled with immortal power. When Hephaestus made him a gift of a silver bow with golden arrows that could not miss their mark, the young god resolved to kill the Python, the monster that had pursued his mother so relentlessly.

Swift as lightning, Apollo flew to Parnassus, where the dreadful monster had its lair. Until that moment, nobody had dared to raise his arm against the Python, which spread unheard-of miseries all around it. Wherever it dragged its serpent's body the earth and all its fruits decayed and a foul rottenness spread over the land, whilst men died immediately they set eyes upon its awful form.

As soon as the fearsome dragon realized that someone had dared to try his strength against it, it came out of its lair and wormed its huge length among the rocks, searching out the enemy. When the monster saw that the being who stood before it was none other than the child of Leto, it went mad with anger and flecks of foam dripped from its mouth in its fury. Raising itself upon its snaky coils the Python loomed threateningly over Apollo, drawing its head back for the lunge that would tear the young god into bloody pieces.

Quicker than lightning, Apollo loosed a single arrow at the Python and hit it straight between the eyes.

A terrifying howl echoed through the mountain gorges as the horrible monster, mortally wounded, beat its writhing scales against the rocky slopes of Mount Parnassus, coiling and then uncoiling to its full length. Suddenly it raised itself, huge and threatening, to its full height only to fall back again with a fearful thud which shook the whole mountain. The Python was dead.

Overjoyed by his great victory, Apollo took up his beloved golden lyre and began to sing the paean of victory.
To the triumph of a heroic feat was added yet another
triumph, a triumph that was no more than a song, but a
song so wonderful the world had never heard its like
before. From its words and music sprang all the contrast
between savage struggle and peace, between destruction
and creation, death and life. It was a song of overwhelming
beauty and power, a song which nature heard in silent awe
and which filled the eyes of oppressed mankind with tears
of trembling happiness.

When Apollo's paean had ended, a mighty clamour rose
up on all sides. It was the tumultuous cheers and delighted
cries of mankind and all nature, their roars of applause at
this triumphant hymn; and ever since, Apollo has rightly
held unchallenged the title of god of music.

Apollo buried the Python on the side of Mount Parnassus and over the monster's grave he built a temple and an
oracle. This was the sacred oracle of Delphi, which reveals
to men the judgements of almighty Zeus, Apollo's father.

The shepherd of king Admetus

The Python, however, was the son of mother Earth, and
in killing it Apollo had become a murderer. Since Apollo
was the very god who would one day hold the power to

absolve repentant killers of their sins, his first duty was to cleanse himself from the guilt of his own crime, even though it had been a blessing to gods and men alike. And so, casting off his immortal form, he went to Thessaly, where he became a humble shepherd in the service of king Admetus of Pherae. Thus the golden-haired youth tended the royal flocks, and nobody, not even Admetus himself, suspected that the young herdsman was Apollo, god of light.

Yet strange things would happen whenever Apollo took his master's herds to graze. Whenever the god picked up his lyre and let his fingers play upon its strings, the wild beasts would come out of the forest as if entranced and gambol around him joyfully, mingling with the cows and sheep. From the time of Apollo's arrival, wealth and happiness began to flow into the courts of Admetus. His flocks multiplied, his store-rooms filled with sacks of grain, and his great urns overflowed with olives and wine, oil and butter. From the walls and roofbeams hung heavy bags of cheese, legs of ham and other foods, all of the choicest quality.

Handsome young Admetus rejoiced in the plenty that he saw around him. Mounted upon his white stallion, he would ride out over the plain, admiring his herds, his sleek and well-muscled horses galloping over the rolling turf and his powerful oxen dragging the plough deep through the fertile soil.

Many kings now wanted Admetus as their son-in-law and offered him their daughters; but he loved only Alcestis, the lovely daughter of Pelias, king of neighbouring Iolchus.

Pelias, however, had no intention of marrying his daughter off, for who else was there to tend him in his old age? So he declared that he would only give his daughter away to a man who could harness a lion and a wild boar to his chariot.

How could anyone yoke together two wild beasts so different and so savage when till now no one had even dared try yoking one alone? Admetus, however, was so emboldened by his love for the sweet Alcestis that he was willing to risk being torn to pieces by the savage beasts. And when Apollo heard of his brave decision, he resolved to help him and gave him the strength he would need to achieve his aim.

Thus the daring Admetus performed the mighty feat Pelias had demanded, and now he was thundering along the road to Iolchus, his chariot harnessed to a lion and a wild boar.

Overcome with awe at the brave young man's incredible feat, Pelias handed over his daughter without protest. Alcestis took her place in the chariot and Admetus brought her in triumph back to his palace, where a sumptuous wedding was celebrated.

Nine years Apollo had bound himself to serve Admetus, and when the ninth year drew to its close the golden-haired god returned to Delphi, purified at last. From then on, Apollo was to be the god of the great and noble ideal of forgiveness, offering his protection to every man who showed sincere and true remorse.

The land beyond the north

Apollo liked to stay at Delphi, where now stood his majestic temple and the sacred oracle. Yet neither did he forget Delos, the island of his birth – and above all he did not forget the promise his mother, Leto, had made before she bore him. For this reason, it was not long before a gleaming temple, built by Apollo, stood out among the other sacred monuments of the island.

But from time to time he would leave Greece to travel to the mythical sunlit land beyond the North where his mother now lived.

Apollo's journeys to this enchanting land were long but wonderful. Mounted on a winged chariot drawn by two great, snow-white swans, he would travel high above the clouds, leaving Greece far behind him. As he travelled further northwards, he would catch sight of the first snows from on high, covering the mountains peaks like white caps. Gradually the snow would grow thicker, until everything beneath Apollo's chariot seemed covered by a white sheet. But above the clouds, where Apollo flew, the weather was always spring-like, and the great swans would draw the chariot onwards swiftly and tirelessly. Finally, even further to the north, the snows would begin to thin out, and far beyond the pole itself golden sunbeams would shine through the clouds, shedding their light upon an enchanted land.

This was the land of the Hyperboreans, the Land Beyond the North. Here was a country of eternal spring, brightly coloured and bathed in cool light; a region echoing with the tinkle of plashing waters and the sweet songs of iridescent birds. As soon as the golden-haired god descended from his chariot and set foot upon the green grass the birds would burst into a frenzied song of welcome and flutter among the branches and the golden shafts of sunlight. So beautifully did they sing that their melody almost rivalled the heavenly notes that Apollo plucked from his lyre.

But at that same moment in distant Greece, clouds would darken the sky. Cold and rain would follow, for the god of light had left his homeland and dark winter was coming in his stead. Huddled around their fires, people would patiently await the return of Apollo and the winter's end. When the god of light came back he would chase away the dark days with his golden beams and bring in the warm and sparkling spring. Then people would hold great feasts to worship the god and sing songs about the sun, the light and the joys of life.

Apollo and Daphne

Apollo loved all life's beauties. One day, at Delphi, he was shooting at targets with his golden arrows. While he was practising, young Eros, the winged son of Aphrodite, arrived on the scene looking for a chance to enmesh Apollo in some affair of the heart.

Seeing that Apollo's arrow had just plunged into an apple hanging from a distant bough, Eros raised his bow and aimed it at the same target.

"Leave me alone, little boy, and let me shoot my arrows," said Apollo in annoyance, "and don't be rash enough to try your skill against mine."

"I know your arrows never miss, but mine, too, hit their mark," replied Eros, even more annoyed than Apollo; and with that he opened his wings and flew up onto the slopes of Mount Parnassus. There he drew two arrows from his quiver – one to arouse love and the other to make the beloved feel only fear and dislike. With the first arrow he wounded Apollo to the heart, and with the second he shot at the nymph Daphne, daughter of the river Peneius, who happened to be passing by at that moment.

Pierced by the dart of love, Apollo was dazzled by the

nymph's lovely face and noble form and went over to speak to her.

Daphne, however, had been struck by the arrow which rejected love, and as soon as she saw Apollo she moved further away. Then the golden-haired god came closer still; but with hasty steps Daphne moved even further from him. With a few quick bounds, Apollo tried once again to approach the lovely nymph. That was enough. Daphne took to her heels. Now Apollo ran after her as if possessed, crying to her to stop; but she ran ever swifter. Both Eros' arrows had found their mark.

"Stop, stop, I beg you," Apollo pleaded. "I don't wish to harm you." But the fleet-footed nymph continually evaded his clutches. However, Apollo did not give up, and kept on running after her and begging her to stop.

"Don't be afraid, lovely nymph!" he called. "Why do you flee as if some wild beast were pursuing you? I am not evil. I am Apollo, the son of Zeus. Stop running like a frightened deer, I beg you!"

But Daphne kept on running. At times Apollo gained on her and it seemed that he would catch her, and at times she would surge ahead with a sudden bound. Then he would be hot on her heels again, reaching out to catch her, but again she would slip from his grasp like a terrified butterfly.

Yet the golden-haired god would not give up his wild pursuit. The dart of love had lit a fire within him which

...With sad eyes he fondled the foliage of the
fragrant laurel...

could not be quenched.

"She can't last out much longer. Sooner or later she will tire and I shall catch her," said Apollo to himself as he kept on running after the nymph.

Sure enough, Daphne eventually began to tire. Apollo drew nearer and nearer to her. Now he was stretching out his hands, now he was about to touch her, now she was almost in his grasp.

"O gods and mother Earth!" gasped Daphne, "why do you let me fall into Apollo's clutches? I do not want Apollo for my husband. I would rather become a rock or a tree than have Apollo touch me."

Hardly had Daphne spoken these words when her feet became rooted to the ground. From her hair and her arms sprang branches and leaves, while her body became the trunk of a tree. Thus the lovely nymph was transformed into a fragrant daphne bush, the familiar laurel of our own times, and instead of embracing her, Apollo found himself clutching an armful of leaves.

The golden-haired god was overcome with sorrow. He was grieved to think that the nymph with whom he had fallen in love so suddenly and so deeply had been lost on his account. With sad eyes, he fondled the foliage of the fragrant laurel and then broke off a spray of leaves to weave a garland for his brow. Apollo was never to forget the lovely and untameable nymph and that is why he is often shown wearing a circlet of laurel leaves on his head.

Apollo and Marpessa

Apollo never married. He was the most handsome of all the gods and lived his life exactly as he pleased. He did promise to marry on one occasion, but even then it was doubtful whether he would have remained faithful, and fortunately the wedding never took place.

The girl was Marpessa, daughter of the king of Aetolia. Her father, Evenus, treated her harshly, but he was a worthy and brave warrior.

He had announced that he would give his daughter only to the man who could beat him in a chariot duel.

Marpessa was so lovely, and her fortune so immense, that at first there were many who found the courage to meet Evenus single-handed; but each had been killed in his turn and now there was no one left who dared to face him — until one day a handsome and daring youth appeared before Marpessa mounted on a winged horse, a pegasus. He was the heroic Idas, son of the king of Messene, and he had never yet been defeated in battle.

Marpessa had heard many tales of Idas' feats and she was appalled when she saw him. Better not to be married at all than be wedded to the man who would slay her father; for now it would not just be any young warrior that Evenus would have to face, but the renowned hero Idas, who could certainly defeat him.

Idas saw the fear in Marpessa's eyes and he said gently:

"Listen, lovely princess. I have not come to kill your father and I want neither his wealth nor his throne. Come, let us leave secretly before day breaks."

When Marpessa heard the noble young man's proposal she was overwhelmed with joy, and immediately agreed to leave with him. He placed her on the back of his splendid pegasus, a gift from Poseidon, and they sped through the air towards Messene.

As soon as king Evenus learned that his daughter had fled with Idas, he called upon Apollo for aid. The god, who loved Marpessa himself, willingly agreed to help, and quick as lightning the two set off together in pursuit of the runaway lovers.

But as they were crossing the river Lycormas, Evenus was swept away by its turbulent waters. Apollo plunged in and dragged him out, but it was too late: Evenus was dead. Apollo swore over the king's body that he would take Marpessa from Idas and make her his wife. He also promised the dead king that although his life had been lost his name would remain immortal, for the river where he had been drowned would henceforth be called the Evenus. Having spoken these words, the god sped off once more in pursuit of Idas; and before the youth could reach the shelter of Messene he found himself face to face with Apollo.

Idas guessed immediately what the god had come for, but instead of retreating he quickly placed himself before Marpessa to shield her, whilst his grim expression showed that he was ready for whatever might come. The young man who had avoided a duel with Evenus, a mere mortal, did not now hesitate to pit his strength against a god. Within moments the two adversaries were locked in struggle.

It was a terrible fight. Although Idas was no god, he was stronger than a lion and he fought against Apollo as an equal. It was not long before Zeus noticed the disturbance, and he decided to part them. However, the two were locked in such furious combat that it seemed impossible to do so, and it was only when the lord of Olympus hurled a thunderbolt between them that he brought the fighting to a halt.

When they had scrambled to their feet, Zeus ordered them to tell him what the quarrel was about.

"Father Zeus," Apollo protested, "I want Marpessa for my wife and this mortal shows great disrespect in daring to stand in my way."

"Father of gods and men," replied Idas, "Marpessa is mine, and nothing will make me give her up."

Zeus stood thoughtfully for a moment and then, turning towards Marpessa, said to her:

"Fair princess, you have every right to choose for your-

self the husband whom you want, and I promise you that
whatever you decide will be fulfilled."

Marpessa humbly thanked great Zeus for his ruling and
then, turning to the god of light, she said:

"Apollo, you are a god and will enjoy eternal youth, but
I shall grow old one day and then you will abandon me.
Lord Zeus, for years I have lived in unhappiness, knowing
that I was destined to be married to my father's killer. Of
all my suitors, only Idas has shown love, discretion and
indomitable courage. I love him and wish to become his
wife."

And so it came about. Apollo submitted to the will of
Zeus, and, filled with admiration for Marpessa's good sense
and Idas' boldness, he wished them every happiness and
departed for Delphi.

Apollo never knew sadness — for did he not have his
lyre, which banished all troubles and brought him calm and
joy? He would often play upon it at the great symposia of
the gods on Olympus. When he touched his fingers to the
magic strings of the golden instrument, the nine Muses
would run joyfully to his side and take up the song, and the
whole place would echo with sweet, immortal melodies.
And when they were in the mood for dancing, the Muses
and the Graces would spring up at once and with them the
lovely Aphrodite; but first in line would be Apollo's sister,

graceful Artemis.

And as spirits rose on Olympus, so unhappiness faded from the earth.

Asclepius

Apollo also had some children, one of whom was Pan, the goat-footed god of the woods; but of him we shall tell in a later book. Another of his sons was the renowned physician, Asclepius.

His mother was Coronis, daughter of the king of Thessaly, but she died as soon as she had given birth to him. Apollo then placed the child in the care of the wisest teacher in the world, the centaur Cheiron who lived on the thickly-wooded slopes of Mount Pelion. Under Cheiron's guidance, Asclepius learned so much of medicine that in the end his knowledge surpassed even that of his teacher. Not only was there no illness he could not cure, but he had even learned the secret of restoring life.

However, this was a blessing men were not destined to enjoy for long, for Pluto, lord of Hades, complained to his brother Zeus about this raising of the dead, fearing that if it continued the Kingdom of the Underworld would soon be emptied.

When the lord of Olympus heard that the dead were being brought back to life, he sprang to his feet in a rage. His

brows darkened, his eyes took on a fierce glint and immediately the sky was filled with black clouds.

Lightning flashed, thunder rolled and the earth began to
shake. It was as if all the heavens were tumbling down.

"Who is he to change the established order and the laws
which govern the world?" roared the lord of gods and men;
and instantly he struck Asclepius down with a thunderbolt
and sent him to the kingdom of Hades.

Apollo was grieved at the loss of his son, but his death
was mourned even more by the mortal men who had
worshipped him above many of the gods.

However, even from the underworld Asclepius still had
the power to help mankind and cure the sick, and all over
Greece there were temples in his honour and other buildings, called "asclepeia", which were a kind of hospital and
were always built in the healthiest spot in each region.
There the priests of Asclepius, who were also physicians,
cured the sick by consultation, with herbal medicines and
through prayer.

Asclepius was helped in his work by his daughters
Hygeia and Panacea. The first of these made sure that
people lived in a healthy way, to avoid illness, whilst the
second was a wonderful pharmacist. She had compounded
a medicine the like of which was nowhere to be found. It,
too, was called the panacea. It was a very rare medicine,

but it cured every disease – or so people said.

HERMES

Hermes steals Apollo's heifers

Now we come to the most devious of the gods, crafty Hermes, the son of Zeus and Maia. Hermes was born in a cave on lofty Mount Cyllene in Arcadia, and as soon as he saw the light of day he began his cunning tricks. As he was a god there was no need for years to pass until he could prove his powers, and so he was up to mischief even before he was out of his cradle.

Nobody knows what Apollo had done to Hermes to put the idea of stealing his cattle into the young god's head. Whatever it was, little Hermes clambered out of his cradle and set off for Piereia where Apollo was tending the herds of the gods of Olympus.

With great stealth and cunning, Hermes managed to rob Apollo of fifty heifers without being seen and to lead them off to the Peloponnese. And what sly means did he not employ to bring his feat to a successful conclusion! Before he had gone very far, he prised the hooves from the heifers' feet and stuck them on again back to front; then he flung his sandals into the sea and quickly made himself another pair with pointed heels and rounded toes. Thus, anyone who followed the marks on the road would think that the herd and the person driving them were going in the direction the footprints showed, whilst it was really quite the opposite.

Further down the road, young Hermes met an old man. Fearing that he might reveal his secret, the little god gave the old man a heifer and told him:

"If you saw something, pretend you saw nothing – and if you heard something, pretend you heard nothing, either.

Agreed?"

"Agreed," replied the old man, more than happy with the heifer he was offered for his pains.

Hermes set off down the road once more, but he was still none too happy about the old man.

"He could give the whole game away," said the young god to himself. "I had better go back and see if he is as good as his word." And so, having hid the heifers in a wood, Hermes transformed himself into a hunter, went back to the old man and said:

"Tell me which way a young boy went with fifty cows, and I shall give you an ox and a heifer."

The old man liked the idea of this second gift and all unsuspecting showed the "hunter" the way they had gone.

"Traitor!" shouted Hermes, "now I'll show you whom you're dealing with!" As he spoke, the earth shook and a huge rock broke loose from the mountainside and flattened the old man beneath it. Believe it or not, the rock was the very image of the old man – except that it could no longer betray confidences!

If ever you go down to the Peloponnese, perhaps you may see a rock whose shape reminds you of that story of the old man. And if it is not the rock which crushed him, then, who knows, perhaps it is at least the rock which gave rise to the legend.

But to return to our story.

After punishing the old man, Hermes went back to the wood, rounded up the herd, and finally drove them to a place near Pylos. There he slaughtered two heifers as an offering to the gods. But where was the fire to roast them on? It didn't take the quick-witted youngster very long to find an answer to that. He took two bone-dry laurel twigs and rubbed them together until they burst into flame. Then he spitted the two heifers and put them on the fire to roast. When they were done, he divided the meat into ten portions and offered one to each of the other gods – except Apollo, of course! Who would dare give him away, now that all Olympus had shared in the spoils? Hermes himself ate nothing; he just sniffed the savoury odours from the roasting meat and that was enough for him.

Once the sacrifice was completed, he hid the remaining heifers in a cave and then went quietly and happily back to his cradle.

As soon as his mother saw him, she began to scold him for having been away all day; but young Hermes was quite unabashed and proudly told her of the cunning trick he had played.

"You silly child," cried Maia, "aren't you afraid of Apollo? Don't you know his arrows never miss their mark? What have you done?"

"I'm not afraid of Apollo," replied the little god, "and if he tries to make a fuss about this, I'll go and loot his temple at Delphi — and then you'll see how everybody laughs at him!"

Apollo, of course, soon realised that his heifers had gone, and began searching for them. On looking around, he quickly found the hoofmarks of the heifers and with them the footprints of a child. He followed them, but saw to his surprise that the marks were leading him back to his starting point. It never occurred to him that a thief could possibly be so cunning, and as he could think of no other way of getting at the truth he decided to consult the oracles. He was the most skilled of all the gods in interpreting them, and it was he who had built the oracle at Delphi. The signs told Apollo that it was Hermes who had stolen his heifers and that they were hidden in a cave near Pylos. Apollo hastened to the spot, and once more found hoofmarks outside the cave and the footprints of the same child. But the marks all showed that the cave was now empty and the heifers had gone.

"He got here before me and took them away," thought Apollo, and, deceived once more by the reversed footprints, he didn't go into the cave at all.

Anxious not to waste another moment, Apollo took a mighty leap and within seconds had reached Cyllene, where he found Hermes lying in his cradle.

"Tell me where you've hidden the heifers!" Apollo roared. "Tell me this very instant or I'll throw you into the darkest depths of Tartarus!"

But what hope was there of getting a straight answer from the cunning little god? Young Hermes just acted like a baby and replied innocently, "Don't expect me to know where they are – I was only born yesterday!"

But Apollo did not believe a word crafty Hermes was saying.

"Get up, you little thief!" he shouted furiously. "I'm taking you off to Zeus this minute. You won't get away with any more of your cunning tricks, just you see!"

Hermes, however, just lay where he was, while Apollo grew more and more angry. Finally, losing all patience, he dragged the baby god from his cradle and carried him off in the direction of Olympus.

"All right, all right," cried Hermes. "There's no need to treat me like this. I didn't say I wouldn't go." And as soon as Apollo had put him down, he added craftily, "And when we get there, you'll see how wrong you were to call me a thief."

They soon found Zeus, but even when faced by the lord of Olympus, his own and Apollo's father, Hermes boldly denied all knowledge of the theft.

"You know yourself," he told Zeus, "that I didn't take Apollo's heifers."

Zeus most certainly did know, and in a stern tone that put a stop to all argument he ordered Hermes to take

Apollo that very instant to the spot where the heifers were hidden.

What else could Hermes do? Zeus was in no mood for joking – so he took Apollo and led him to the cave near Pylos.

Apollo looked down and once more saw the hoofmarks which showed that the heifers had gone. He turned to Hermes with a suspicious look and said,

"I see you're still trying to pull the wool over my eyes." Then he lost his temper and shouted:

"Take me to the place where you've really hidden those heifers or I'll..."

"Calm down, calm down!" Hermes told him in a sooth- ing tone, "and come inside." And taking Apollo by the hand he led him into the cave.

Apollo could hardly believe his eyes when he saw the herd standing there. Who would have believed such cun- ning existed? To be fooled by a babe in arms!

Scarlet with wounded pride and rage, Apollo could hardly keep his hands from the little god, but Hermes, behaving as if nothing had happened, picked up a strangely-shaped lyre and began to play a melody of such beauty that the infuriated Apollo, who was, remember, the god of music, immediately forgot to be angry and listened as if spellbound.

"What heavenly notes come from this strange instrument!" he marvelled. "What Muse is this that calms all passions and dispels anger with such ease?"

But if the music had moved Apollo, it exerted an even greater influence upon Hermes himself. He felt a change take place within him. He now felt ashamed of his crafty behaviour and said:

"I shouldn't have done that to you."

Then he offered Apollo his lyre and added, "Please take this lyre to show that you're not still angry with me. I made it with my own hands. I took an empty tortoise shell and fixed these strings to it. You heard how beautifully it plays!"

For the god of music this was the most precious gift he could have wished for. So great was Apollo's joy that he swore that none of the immortal gods would ever be so dear to him as Hermes.

Their joy was mutual; for when Hermes gave his lyre to Apollo he felt as if he were giving him a part of himself. The feeling made him very happy, for he knew that friendship is won by giving.

When the time came for them to part, Apollo stood in thought for a moment and then said:

"Hermes, take the heifers. I want you to have them as a gift. Please, if you want to seal our friendship, don't refuse them."

And so they parted, delighted with the exchange.

...Friendship is won by giving...

Hermes, a cunning god

Thus ended Hermes' first wicked prank. Yet it was not to be the only one, for the young god simply could not stay out of mischief. Once he took Poseidon's trident and hid it; another time he stole Ares' sword; and once he even dared to hide his father's sceptre. If Zeus hadn't found it almost immediately who knows on whom he would have vented his anger.

Once however, when he was still a boy, Hermes learnt a painful lesson. He went to steal his father's thunderbolts, but as soon as he laid hands on them they burst into flame. There were great rolls of thunder and flashes of lightning. Young Hermes burnt his fingers and cried out in panic at the noise. But the crash of the thunderclaps was nothing to his father's angry roars. Hermes realised that he had done wrong and was thoroughly ashamed of having made such a fool of himself.

However, Hermes could also put his cunning to good use. In an earlier chapter we saw him steal back Zeus' tendons from the Typhoon and thread them into his father's hands and feet again, thus helping him to defeat the hideous monster.

The truth is that nobody could surpass Hermes in cunning, intelligence and swiftness. He had wings on his ankles and could fly to the furthest corners of the earth in a matter of seconds.

For this reason he was the messenger of the gods and at the special command of Zeus, who made frequent use of his abilities and assigned him the most difficult tasks. But whatever the lord of Olympus had set him to do, the quick-witted Hermes never had any difficulty in accomplishing the mission he had undertaken.

Being a wily god, Hermes had a special affection for wily men, and for this reason he was the patron of merchants and lawyers, who are well known for their guileful ways. With his herald's staff he bestowed wealth and happiness on those under his protection.

It was even said that he shielded thieves, but many of them came to an evil end, and then they blamed Hermes for leaving them to their fate.

Hermes also protected labourers, farm workers and especially shepherds, since, as we have seen, he acquired a herd of his own when he was still only a baby. Even the hat he wore was a herdsman's cap on which he had fastened wings.

As he was young, handsome and strongly built, Hermes loved field sports. He was the patron of athletes and made sure that the rules were observed in all contests. This was why statues of Hermes were to be found by every running track.

At crossroads and half-way points along the main routes,

travellers would come upon busts of Hermes mounted on pillars. There they could rest secure in the knowledge of his protection – for no robber would dare to attack a traveller resting at the foot of one of Hermes' columns.

These columns had useful information for travellers inscribed upon them, which was of great assistance to any who had not been along the road before. There was also a thoughtful custom of leaving a little food for hungry travellers at their base.

In spite of his crafty tricks and his sly ways, Hermes was one of the most popular of gods with mortals and Olympians alike. There were many who even admired him for his little weaknesses, but he wanted people to be intelligent and clear-thinking, and to those who were he showed especial favour.

The water of oblivion

Hermes' quick mind and supple form made him the favourite of the wood-nymphs. One of the nymphs of Sicily bore him a son, but she was a heartless mother and abandoned her child in a grove of laurels, or "daphnes" as they are called in Greek.

Some kind water-nymphs found the baby among the laurels. They named him Daphnis, and brought him up with loving care to be a fine shepherd. Daphnis had a deep love

...Daphnis was taught to play the pipes by Pan, the
goat-footed god of the woods...

of music and was taught to play the pipes by Pan, the goat-footed god of the woods. Daphnis made up his own songs and composed his own melodies, which he sang and played on the pan-pipes.

In his verses he told of the life of the shepherd and the beauty of the forests and mountain pastures and thus he became the first pastoral poet. Hermes was very fond of his son Daphnis, for he was a young man who brought credit to his father's name and became known the world over for the melodies he played and the poems which he set to music.

This handsome and noble shepherd was loved by the nymph Lyce and they became the happiest and best matched couple in the whole of Sicily. For Lyce, too, had a lovely, sweet voice and when she sang and he played on the pipes it was as if some muse from Olympus were singing and Pan himself were playing.

Yet although there was nothing to cast a shadow on their happiness, Lyce fell prey to a great fear – the fear that she would lose her beloved.

"Daphnis, dearest," she said, "the happier I feel, the more afraid I become. There are times when I can see our happiness collapsing in ruins. I am afraid of losing you, Daphnis, and I would rather die than have such a thing happen."

"Dearest love," replied Daphnis, "only the gods know our fate. If I should die, pray for a brave heart and struggle to live on; but for me to forget you while I live, why, that's impossible. I swear before the gods that I would let you blind me with your own hands if ever I should leave you for the sake of another woman."

Yet fate decreed that the very next day the impossible should happen.

Daphnis had gone out hunting, and, tired by the chase, sat down upon a stone to rest. Then he took up his pan-pipes and began to play a melody. Nearby, hidden behind the thick foliage of the forest trees, was a splendid palace. A gentle breeze wafted the sweet notes of Daphnis' pipes straight to the open window of the princess who sat there listening, enchanted by the beauty of music. When the last notes of the pipes had died away, the princess ran down the steps and stood in the palace gateway, hoping to catch sight of the musician. Meanwhile, Daphnis had got to his feet and had gone on through the forest in the mid-day heat, searching for water. Suddenly without realising it, he found himself before the palace gates, looking full in the face of the king's daughter, who had come forward at that very moment.

When she saw the handsome youth with his pipes, the princess fell in love with him on the spot and asked him to come up to the palace.

"Just bring me a little water to quench my thirst," replied Daphnis, "and then I'll be on my way, fair princess, for I am out past my time and my beloved awaits my return."

The princess, however, was no ordinary woman. She was well-versed in sorcery and into his water she poured a few drops of juice from the magic herb of forgetfulness.

She then came back to the gates and stretched out her arm with a smile to hand Daphnis the drink.

At that moment a sudden breeze blew up. The leaves rustled on the trees and in their murmuring it seemed as if a voice could be heard:

"No, Daphnis! Don't drink it! Don't you see her eyes? They are the eyes of a witch, Daphnis!"

But the young man's ears were filled with the sound of tinkling waters and he stretched out both hands to the cup.

"Daphnis! No, Daphnis!" came the voice again. "Do not drink the water of oblivion or you will forget us!"

"It must be the wind," said Daphnis to himself. "There's nobody here but the princess and me, and besides, I'm hot and thirsty and I want a drink." And tossing back his parched throat he emptied the cup in one draught.

Thus Daphnis quenched his thirst – and thus he forgot the girl he loved, his vow to the gods and everything else.

Taking him by the hand, the princess led him into the palace.

Lyce awaited his return in vain. Hour after hour went by, and then, desperate with anxiety, she began to search for him high and low. Eventually, quite by chance, she found herself outside the gates of the palace. Two guards stood there.

"I am looking for Daphnis, the singer with the pan-pipes," sobbed Lyce. "Have you seen him pass this way, by any chance?"

"Don't ask for Daphnis again. He is the princess's lover now, so forget him just as he has forgotten you," replied one of the guards, realising who Lyce was.

Like a mad creature, the nymph burst into the palace. Before anyone had time to stop her she was face to face with Daphnis.

Daphnis met her look. It was as if he had been struck by a thunderbolt which woke him from a dreadful nightmare.

"Lyce..." he stammered.

"The vow, the vow, o gods!" cried Lyce — and her eyes burned into the young man's as if they were flashing fire.

As Daphnis stared at her, his eyes opened wide in terror and as they did so, pains began to shoot through them. Soon the agony was unbearable, and instinctively he closed his eyes. When he opened them again he could no longer see.

Now Daphnis was blind, and he picked his uncertain way through the woods playing sad melodies on his pipes and singing of the sweetest happiness in the world, which had turned into the bitterest sorrow.

Whilst wandering aimlessly one day, groping his way in

the pitch darkness of high noon, he fell from a rock and was killed.

Hermes found his son as the breath was leaving his body, and carried him off to Olympus. And there at the foot of the rock, on the spot where he fell, a spring gushed forth. To this very day the people of Sicily point out this spring and say that in the plashing of its waters the pipes of Daphnis can be heard.

DEMETER

The goddess of agriculture

The story of Demeter begins in the days when the terrible war against the Titans had just come to an end. After the bitterest fighting the world had ever seen, Zeus and the gods of Olympus had toppled the fearsome Titans from their thrones and become the new lords of the earth.

In the aftermath of such a war, the victors were beset with a host of serious problems. The most pressing of these was to save the human race from the hunger which was slowly wiping it out.

Those ten long years of fearful war had ravaged the whole earth. Not a blade of green was left, and those few

men who had survived wandered in starving bands, begging the gods for help. Zeus was now the lord of earth and
sky, and in his desire to help mankind, he made the goddess
Demeter responsible for all the plains and forests in the
world. It would be her task to see that the earth bore fruit so
that both men and animals should have enough to eat.

The mighty Zeus had made a wise choice. No one loved
the green meadows and the placid herds with the same
passion as did Demeter – and her greatest love was for
mankind. She threw herself into the difficult task with
enthusiasm. The meadows were soon carpeted with green,
and fruit hung from the boughs. No longer faced with
immediate starvation, mankind slowly began to multiply.
But this was not enough for the gentle goddess.

In those distant times, man had not yet learned to farm
the land. He lived in the forest like a wild creature, struggling against savage beasts and the wildness of nature. His
home was a cave or a makeshift shelter of branches and his
only food the fruit he picked wild from the trees or the
occasional animal he managed to kill in the chase.

He and his kind were obliged to wander from place to
place, for when there was no food left in one spot they had
to search elsewhere for more. Often, however, there was
nothing to be found and they were ravaged by hunger. At
other times, when out collecting food or hunting, they
would run into men of another tribe. Then there was no

choice but to give battle: a savage blood-bath to decide who had the right to gather a few wild berries, or to go hunting in that particular part of the forest.

It wounded the goddess to the heart to see man suffer so. Something had to be done. She had to find some way of helping more effectively. The shady woods and the wild meadows were beautiful, but they could not always satisfy man's hunger. His way of life would have to be changed.

Then one day, quite suddenly, as Demeter was sitting on a rock and gazing thoughtfully out over the green plain, a thought flashed into her mind. It was the answer to the problem which had been troubling her for so long.

"Yes, that is what I shall do!" she cried. "I shall teach them to till the soil!" She jumped up and began to walk excitedly to and fro, springing into the air and clapping her hands with joy, like a little child bursting to tell the happiest news in the world. Her thoughts took wing, and the further they flew, the greater her joy became.

"What wonderful changes this will bring to men's lives. Once they have learned to cultivate the land, they will have fields; once they have fields, they will stop wandering from place to place. They will build houses and villages; they will have shelter, gardens and animals of their own. In time, they will learn arts and letters; they will build splendid cities and..... yes! they will no longer need to fight among themselves, for each one will have his own field and his own homeland. What a wonderful chain of events! How much can happen if men learn to till the soil. How happy I am!"

The kind goddess had no time to waste. She hastily disguised herself as an ordinary woman, came down to earth and set to work. And a hard task it was. It was by no means easy to make people understand. Time and time again she planted, dug and watered, single-handed, showing people her work and all the time explaining patiently. But what difficulties she faced! There were many who mocked her, people who were really ignorant but thought they knew everything. She was mad, they said. If this was how the gods had made the world, it wasn't likely to change. But the wiser ones watched her carefully. They sensed their lack of knowledge, realised they were learning new skills and threw themselves whole-heartedly into the task.

Their reward was not slow to come. How much more abundant was the harvest now that it came from seed they had sown themselves! How much more satisfaction they gained from a field watered with the sweat of their own brow, its ears of corn bending under their own weight!

It was now quite clear which way was right, and little by little everybody began to cultivate the soil. They gave up wandering through the forest in search of roots and berries. People now started to build houses, gather in villages and tend herds. They learned arts and letters, built cities and embellished them with temples and statues. So, civilisation came – and with it would also have come lasting peace, had not Ares, the bloodthirsty god of war, not continually incited men to battle. Yet now he found his task more difficult, for the new way of life had made men hate war as the greatest curse ever visited upon the world.

Helped by Eirene, the goddess of peace, Demeter stood constantly on the watch to frustrate Ares' attempts to spread war, and there were often times when long periods of peace reigned upon the earth. Civilisation flourished, and Demeter was happy. Yet whenever Ares achieved his aims and war flared up among mankind, she grieved to see the destruction of work that had taken tens or even hundreds or years to achieve.

The loss of Persephone

"True happiness is beyond the reach of gods and men alike. One day all may be well, and the next everything is in ruins." Demeter had often had such gloomy thoughts, but this time a persistent foreboding nagged at her mind as she wandered sadly over the gentle foothills of Olympus. At last, she sat down on a rock looking out over the rich greenery which stretched away before her; but her eyes were vague, and her face troubled. Suddenly, her thoughts flew to her daughter, Persephone, and her anxiety swelled to anguish. Persephone was her only child, and she loved her more dearly than any other creature in the world.

"Some harm has come to her," the goddess cried, springing up as if she had been struck. Immediately, a furious wind began to howl and whistle. Then a heart-rending cry drowned the roar of the wind and pierced Demeter's ears: "Mother, they are taking me away!" — a terrible, despairing cry, reaching Olympus from far away over the mountains and the seas. It was uttered only once, yet a reverberating echo followed it and brought it back again and again. As it passed through gorges and over mountains and mingled with the whistling of the wind, so its note changed. Sometimes it sounded like a shriek and sometimes like a sob, sometimes it re-echoed and at others it sank to a faint whisper. The goddess' head was swimming and her heart ready to burst with anguish. "Mother, they are taking me away!" It was the voice of her only daughter, Persephone.

Had a thousand thunderbolts struck the goddess they would not have shaken her as much as the cry she heard. Nothing could keep her on Olympus a moment longer. She rose like a startled bird and ran in search of her daughter, her feet sometimes resting on dry land, sometimes on the waves.

"Persephone, Persephone!" she shouted. She ran, crying and searching, in all directions, until her footsteps at last brought her to the flowery vale of Nysa. There she found a group of water-nymphs, the beautiful Oceanides, who had been Persephone's best friends. The goddess ran anxiously towards them, but their eyes seemed to hold no good news for her.

"Quickly, good maidens," she cried, "tell me – what has become of my daughter? Who has snatched her away?"

"Unhappy goddess," came the reply, "we know nothing; we only heard her cry. She was here with us gathering flowers. Look, here are our baskets. We didn't realise that she had wandered away from us. Then we heard a cry – and that was all."

Demeter did not wait to hear any more. With tears streaming down her face, she ran off to continue her search. For nine days and nine nights she went on looking, but all was in vain; whoever she asked, simple mortal or mighty seer, the answer was the same. They knew nothing.

On the evening of the tenth day, when the new moon rose into the sky, Hecate the moon-goddess appeared before Demeter and said: "I have seen your suffering and I have come to help you. Since nobody else knows anything of your daughter, let me take you to Helios, the god of the sun, for he alone among gods and mortals can have seen your daughter snatched away."

The two goddesses soon reached the golden courts of the sun, and stood dazzled before the great god of the day.

When the sun saw Demeter, he knew why she had come. "Dear goddess," he said, "I share your sorrow at the misfortune which has befallen you. What has happened to Persephone, however, was the will of her father, Zeus. He gave her to Pluto, lord of Hades, to be his bride. She is now in the Kingdom of the Underworld, and will never again see the light of day."

When Demeter heard these words, her face turned pale as wax and floods of tears gushed from her eyes, but the sun had more to tell: "Persephone was playing and gathering flowers with her friends, the Oceanides, in the flowery vale of Nysa. It was a beautiful spot, with its green trees and sweet-smelling blooms, its warbling birds and laughing waters. Drunk with the beauty of it all, Persephone flitted like a butterfly from flower to flower, not realising how far behind she had left her friends. But while she was delighting in the beauty of the spot, without a care in the world, Pluto, the lord of Hades, was lying in wait nearby, hidden in a crack in the earth. Suddenly, Persephone caught sight of a lovely narcissus, whose petals were just opening. She picked it and held it to her face to smell its delicate fragrance. Persephone had always been a lovely girl, but in that moment she was lovelier than ever. Pluto, who had watched the whole scene, could restrain himself no longer. With a single blow he split the earth asunder and lunged forward into the daylight upon his golden chariot, drawn by

...In a flash he had dragged Persephone up
beside him!...

the immortal, coal-black horses of Hades. In a flash, he had dragged Persephone up beside him. She scarcely had time to sob, "mother, they are taking me away," before the horses plunged back into the dark earth, blinded by the light of day.

The sun god saw that as his tale unfolded, so Demeter's misery deepened. He tried to comfort her. "Do not grieve," he said, "Pluto is a great lord, and the Kingdom of the Underworld is boundless, for the dead far outnumber the living. Your daughter will live in courts of gold and countless shades of the dead will honour and worship her just as they worship the immortal Pluto, brother of almighty Zeus, who numbers you among his sisters."

But these words only increased Demeter's grief, for she saw that she had lost all that was dearest to her in the world – her only daughter.

Everything was clear to her now, and the pain of her knowledge ruined not only her life but all the beauty she had created. Now, nothing would grow on earth and a frozen north wind raged, stripping the dying leaves from the trees and whirling them through the air.

Gone were the lovely flowers and the green grass. Gone were the rich ears and the sweet fruit. Nothing was left. People, animals and birds began to grow hungry and cold and many of them died. Cries of mourning could be heard on all sides.

Everybody begged Demeter to make the earth green again, to make the trees bear fruit and to bring a smile back to the face of the world, but Demeter's grief was so deep that it made her deaf to all cries and blind to all tragedies but her own.

She was so angry with Zeus for giving their daughter to Pluto without considering her maternal feelings that she never wanted to see Olympus again. Like a mortal mother sorrowing for her lost one, she stumbled blindly over the face of the earth crying and wailing.

In the course of her wanderings, she eventually arrived before the gates of Eleusis. In that spot there stands a well — 'the well of the maidens'— which still exists today. Exhausted, Demeter drank a little water and then sat down upon a large stone, which has been called 'the wailing stone' ever since. The goddess had been sitting there for some hours, buried in her grief, when she was found by four girls who had come for water. They were filled with pity at the sight of this weeping woman in black, and they asked her who she was and what they could do to help her.

"My name is Dio," Demeter replied, not wishing to reveal her true identity. "I come from Crete and I was carried away by pirates, but I managed to escape them, and since then I have been wandering from place to place. Now, I have no idea where I am. If you are from a rich and kind family, as you seem to be, I am good at many kinds of work. I know how to bring up children, how to care for the aged and how to set the serving-girls their various tasks."

"We are the daughters of Celeus, king of Eleusis," the eldest of the girls replied. "Come with us, and we shall take you to our mother, Queen Metaneira. She needs a sensible woman to look after our baby brother, little Demophon." And so they took the stranger to the palace.

As soon as Demeter crossed the threshold, however, the whole palace was flooded with divine light. An astonished Metaneira rose to greet the visitor and to offer her royal throne, for she realised that this was no ordinary mortal. Demeter, however, refused to be seated and remained sadly standing there until Iambe, the queen's hand-maiden, brought a stool for her.

Seeing Demeter's sad face, Iambe began to tell jokes to try and make her laugh. She made such funny faces and so many amusing gestures that a smile finally appeared on Demeter's lips and she accepted a cup of wine. For the first time since the loss of her daughter Persephone, a little happiness had come into her heart.

Demeter stayed at the palace of Celeus, and Metaneira gave the goddess her newly-born son Demophon to nurse. Wishing to reward the royal couple for the kindness they had shown her, Demeter decided to make the baby immortal. First she took the child into her arms and breathed her divine breath into his lungs, then she anointed his body with ambrosia and secretly placed him in a lighted furnace at night, to make his body everlasting. Unluckily, Metaneira saw her doing this, and thinking that Demeter had gone mad she let out such screams that she alarmed the goddess, who took the baby out of the oven and gave it back to the queen saying: "Take your child and look after him yourself from now on. I had hoped to make him into a being that would never know old age and death, and would be honoured for ever. Know that I am the goddess Demeter, and that I wished to thank you for all that you have done for me."

As soon as Demeter revealed her identity, the same divine light again flooded the palace, and the goddess once more appeared in all her former glory. Metaneira and Celeus knelt before her and Demeter commanded the king to build her a temple near the spring of Callirrhoe, at Eleusis. And there, far from Olympus, the unhappy goddess made her home.

In the meantime, however, the earth had become a desert where both men and animals were dying of starvation. Only around Eleusis could a little greenery still be found and it was feared that this, too, would disappear.

Zeus saw all this and realised that he must do something to repair the harm which had been done. He decided that Persephone must return to earth for half the year to live with her mother and live with her husband Pluto for the remainder of the year in the Kingdom of the Underworld. And that is exactly what happened.

Ever since then, in spring and summer the mountains and the plains are clothed in green and the earth garlanded with flowers. All nature rejoices, for these are the seasons when Persephone is at her mother's side; and Demeter, too, in her joy sees to it that the earth is both lovely and fertile. But when Persephone leaves, then the autumn comes, and the cold winter. The leaves fall from the trees and all is miserable and gloomy, for Demeter, too, is sad that her only daughter is far from the light of day, in the inky blackness of Hades.

And so it has continued: every spring Demeter welcomes her beloved daughter back, and in her happiness throws herself into her favourite task, trying to sweeten the painful life of man.

Triptolemus in Scythia

However, not everybody had yet learned how to cultivate the earth. In distant parts of the world men still lived like savages, just as in the old days.

This was how people lived in Scythia, which was then ruled by King Lyngus. Demeter decided to send a hero there, a man who would scorn all dangers in his efforts to teach men the agriculture which would bring them civilisation. The man best fitted for the task, she felt, was Triptolemus, the eldest son of King Celeus.

Demeter gave her hero a winged chariot and two dragons to shield him from evil powers, and he set out for distant Scythia. His strongest protection, however, was his own brave heart.

This fearless hero faced many terrible dangers, but he overcame them all with his sword and finally taught the Scythians how to cultivate the soil. Thus peace slowly came to that people and their land.

King Lyngus, however, was far from satisfied. He was jealous of Triptolemus and made up his mind to kill him and then spread the word that it was he, Lyngus, who had brought the art of agriculture to his people.

But how was he to rid himself of Triptolemus, who killed everybody sent to murder him? Finally, he decided to do the deed himself. Since he did not want to meet the same fate as the others, he decided to commit the crime while Triptolemus was sleeping — yet how could he do so when the hero was guarded in his sleep by the winged dragons Demeter had given him?

In the end, he hit upon a devilish plan. He invited Triptolemus to his palace and served him a splendid feast accompanied by choice wines. He thanked him for the great services he had performed for Scythia and then led him into one of the chambers of the palace to sleep.

Late that night, while Triptolemus was slumbering deeply, Lyngus crept into his room clutching a sharp-pointed dagger. "Ha! The plan has worked!" said Lyngus to himself, but at the very moment when he was raising the dagger, he felt his wrist caught in a vice-like grip. The knife fell to the ground. The terrified Lyngus turned his head and found himself face to face with the goddess Demeter.

"Lyngus, you have sealed your own fate," the goddess hissed. "A swine you are and a swine you shall remain for ever. And immediately the king was transformed into a wild boar which fled panic-stricken into the forest, while Triptolemus left Scythia unharmed, to bring Demeter's gift of agriculture to the other backward peoples of the world. From then on, woe betide anyone who dared to lay a finger on the goddess' fearless favourite.

Erysichthon, murderer of trees

Demeter's task was a sacred one, and all who tried to frustrate or destroy her work had to be punished severely; but the harshest punishment of all was dealt to Erysichthon, the king of Thessaly, the man who wantonly cut down trees.

This, too, is a myth of course, but a very useful one. Forests were no less valuable to man in those days than they are today. It was an evil deed to cut down a tree, for people believed that in every tree there dwelt a nymph, called a dryad – and that dryad would live only as long as the tree itself.

Whoever wished to cut a tree down had to think very seriously before he did so, for Demeter loved and protected the dryads. There was not a man in Greece who did not know this and Erysichthon, being a king, should certainly have known the wishes of the gods even better than an ordinary man. Yet while he should have tried to save the forests, his craving for luxury blinded him to his duty and he cut down trees pitilessly, merely to build himself a new palace.

He went beyond all bounds, however, when his eye fell upon a hundred-year old oak which stood at the entrance to the sacred grove.

When the king arrived with his courtiers before the sacred tree, the whole group stood silent and hesitant. Finally, the eldest of them came forward and said to the king, "Your Majesty, haven't you done enough damage to the forest, building this new palace of yours? Wasn't your old palace beautiful enough? Listen to a word of advice: beauty is something which everyone admires; luxury is not. Try to understand that, and don't cut down the tree. For your own sake, pity the dryad that lives there, for Demeter..."

But Erysichthon cut him short: "Keep your advice to

yourself, old man, and don't think your white hair will
protect you. What do I care about dryads or about Demeter? I am protected by stronger gods. Even if Demeter
herself lived in this oak tree, I would still cut it down!"
With these words, he seized an axe from a slave and furiously began chopping at the noble oak. Immediately he did
so, a miracle occurred. Blood spurted from the wounded
trunk! The onlookers were horrified, and a slave tried to
hold the king back. Erysichthon turned on the man in fury
and killed him, shouting: "There, you dog, I'll teach you to
warn me about Demeter!" And with these words he renewed his attack upon the tree until it toppled beneath his
blows and the dryad in it died.

Now, that dryad had been more dearly loved than any
other in the grove, and her sisters ran in tears to Demeter
and told her of the terrible thing which had happened.

"See what he did, the beast," they cried, "and hear what
he said about you, mighty goddess! — 'Even if Demeter
herself lived in that oak I would still cut it down,' he
snarled — and, 'You dog, I'll teach you to warn me about
Demeter!' — and then he killed the poor slave and cut down
the tree and we lost the best friend we had."

The goddess was furious when she heard these words,
and immediately thought of a punishment to fit the hideous
crime. Now it was the turn of Erysichthon to be pitied — if
such men can be said to deserve any pity.

This is how he was punished.

Demeter ordered a dryad to go to the distant Caucasus and seek out Peina, the goddess of hunger. The dryad was to tell her that by Demeter's command she should go to Erysichthon and breathe her affliction into his body.

In an instant, the dryad had reached the Caucasus and found the goddess of hunger in a cave on a dry, thorny mountainside.

Hunger was bony, haggard and tousle-haired. Her robe was black, and her eyes were sunk deep in their sockets. The dryad recoiled in horror when she saw her, but she soon got her courage back and told her why she had come to the Caucasus.

The goddess of hunger obeyed Demeter's command upon the instant, and carried by a whirlwind, she soon reached the palace of Erysichthon. Night had long since fallen and she found him fast asleep. Hunger covered him with her wings and breathed her poisoned breath upon his face. That was all. Immediately afterwards she disappeared at the same wild speed with which she had come.

And then something strange happened. Although Erysichthon was still fast asleep, his jaws began to open and close because he could see food in his sleep; and although there was nothing in his mouth, he started chewing and swallowing. Suddenly the king woke up, hunger gnawing at his entrails. He roused his servants immediately and bellowed at them to scour the land, drag the seas and empty the skies, and to place whatever they could find to eat before him.

He gulped food down without pausing for breath, yet the more he ate, the more he complained of his hunger. His slaves brought him dish after dish spilling over with food and all the while he shouted that it was too little and sent them back for more. Food that would have sufficed to feed whole nations was not enough to fill his stomach. The harder he chewed and swallowed, the sharper his hunger grew.

His stomach was like a bottomless pit: the more he tried to fill it, the emptier it seemed; insatiable pangs of hunger tore at his entrails and tortured him all the more. And so his whole fortune disappeared into his stomach without being able to quench the fires that burned there. Finally, when he had gobbled up all his wealth, lost his kingdom and his followers and sold his last slave, he found himself left with nothing but his daughter, Mistra, who pitied him although she surely deserved a better father.

This Mistra was so beautiful that the sea-god himself, Poseidon, had once fallen in love with her. Now her father, unable to resist his appetite, sold her too. While on her way to slavery, however, Mistra begged Poseidon for his help, and the sea-god, who still loved her, bestowed on her the power to change herself into any form she wished. So

Mistra became a bird and immediately flew back to her father. And he sold her again. She became a horse and returned once more. And again he sold her. And so she became a heifer, and then a doe and so it went on until finally, having changed herself into a roe-deer, she found herself faced by a flood-swollen river which she could not cross.

Then Erysichthon could no longer control himself. He fell ravenously upon his own flesh and died in horrible agony.

Thus died the man who killed trees; and thus Demeter protected her good works from a few evil men, by showing that hunger awaits those who destroy her woodlands.

Most people, however, loved the trees and the green plains. They loved their work on the land and honoured the goddess Demeter at great festivals. One of these was the Eleusinian Mysteries, which was among the greatest feasts of the year.

This festival, which took place every spring, was a gay celebration at which men honoured Demeter and welcomed the return of her daughter Persephone before throwing themselves into the year's work in the fields, as the goddess of agriculture had taught them.

ARTEMIS

A proud goddess

In the far distant past, on nights when Zeus had retired to rest and the full moon shone bright in the starry sky, a happy party of beautiful nereids would wander through the woods. A tall, lithe maiden stood out amongst them, the most beautiful of them all. All the others obeyed her, and when the group made merry in some clearing in the woods she always proved herself the finest singer and dancer. Her name was Artemis; she was the goddess of moonlit nights and the great queen of the forests.

She wore a short smock which emphasised the divine

grace of her body, and when the silvery beams of the moon fell upon her, she radiated mythical beauty and imposing dignity. She loved hunting and often carried a gilded bow, while from her shoulder hung a golden quiver, filled with arrows which always shot true.

Artemis was the daughter of the mighty Zeus and of the goddess Leto. She was the twin sister of golden-haired Apollo, and in an earlier chapter we saw what sufferings Leto went through before she bore her two children. Artemis loved her mother and the other gods of Olympus. She was bold and proud, and woe betide any who slighted her or any other goddess. When, in spite of this, the two giant Aloades once dared to insult her, Artemis scorned their mighty strength and gave them the punishment they deserved.

Otus and Ephialtes, as they were called, were the two sons of the giant Aloeus. Every year, they grew one fathom in height and one cubit in width. As their size increased, so did their strength – and not only their strength, but their insolence. Mere mortals were of no consequence to them, and these they killed simply for pleasure. Finally, however, they became so bold that they even began to threaten the gods of Olympus.

"Wait till we have grown a little taller," they said, "and we shall pile Mount Pelion on Mount Ossa and reach to the very heavens themselves – and then we shall snatch Hera and Artemis away from you!"

The gods certainly had cause to fear this pair. For had they not chained Ares, the fearsome god of war, and kept him hidden away for thirteen months? What troubled the gods even more was that these two giants had been born virtually immortal, and neither god nor man could kill them. Fate had decreed that they would die only if the one killed the other. Yet how could such an end overtake the two Aloades, whose ambitions bound them together even more firmly than the brotherly blood which flowed in their veins?

Artemis, however, had laid her plans. One day, when the two Aloades went out hunting, the goddess trailed them. The two giants were lying in ambush near each other, waiting for a deer to cross their path. The goddess caught a doe and then released it in a spot where it would pass directly between the two brothers. As soon as Otus and Ephialtes saw the doe, they both took aim immediately. They bent back their bows with all their strength and loosed their shafts like lightning-bolts. The goddess, however, made sure that they missed the doe, and since the target they were aiming at lay exactly between them, their arrows drove home full force into each other's foreheads. Artemis' plan had succeeded: the two Aloades fell dead. There was indescribable joy when the news of the terrible giants' end became known, and everybody sang hymns of praise to

Artemis in honour of her great achievement.

Hippolytus and Phaedra

In Greece, Artemis was also widely worshipped as the goddess of chastity, and along with her they honoured Hippolytus, a handsome young man who dedicated his life to the service of the goddess and by his death became the symbol of upright and honourable youth.

Hippolytus was the son of the hero Theseus, king of Athens. His mother was the lovely Antiope, queen of the Amazons, who fell at Theseus' side fighting bravely in the defence of Athens. Theseus later remarried; his second wife was Phaedra, daughter of the famous king of Crete, Minos.

After the king's second marriage, Hippolytus left Athens and went to the Peloponnese where he stayed with his great-grandfather, the sage Pittheus. Pittheus, who was king of Troezen, made the young man heir to his throne.

Hippolytus had inherited two qualities from his Amazonian mother: a love of horses and a deep-rooted adoration for the goddess Artemis. Four splendid steeds drew his chariot, which he controlled with breath-taking skill. He took part in the Olympic games, and when he returned victorious to Troezen, standing upright upon his chariot, the young people of the town ran to greet him as if he were a god from Olympus.

Yet far more important in the young man's life was his worship of the goddess Artemis as the symbol of the purity of youth. He spent the greater part of his time in the goddess' sacred grove, and he had become the dearest person in the world to her. The son of Theseus was the only mortal the goddess would meet and speak with. Together they hunted deer and wild boar, together they drank crystal-clear water from shady springs and together they rode in company, side by side. Artemis' love for Hippolytus was deep, chaste and sisterly, and his love for the goddess was filled with respect, worship and purity.

However, Aphrodite, the goddess of love, felt insulted by the fervour Hippolytus showed in his worship of Artemis. She could not bear to see him pass her statue without even stopping to beg a favour or to lay an offering at her feet.

"What right," she cried, "has he to ride at her side day after day? Mortals were created to worship all the gods of Olympus, and not just one alone!" And with these words, she waited for her chance to strike.

Now one day, Hippolytus went to Athens to attend a religious ceremony at his father's palace. Aphrodite knew that there he would meet his step-mother, Phaedra, and that this woman would be the most suitable person to use as a tool to bring about the young man's destruction. One shaft from the bow of her winged son, Eros, was all Aphrodite needed to make Phaedra forget her love for her husband and feel passionate longing for the noble youth. Sure enough, when the queen of Athens set eyes upon the lithe young figure of Hippolytus, her heart beat faster. Alarmed by her feelings, she tried to bring herself to her senses and think of the harm she would do to her husband, but it was impossible to listen to the voice of reason. The most she could do was to prevent herself from speaking to Hippolytus.

Once the young man had left, Phaedra could find no peace. She was unable to sleep or eat and became thin and pale. One day, impatient to see Hippolytus again, she went to Troezen. There, she hid in the temple of Aphrodite or 'The Temple of the Secret Watcher' as it has been called ever since. From her hiding-place, she could see the young man in the distance as he performed gymnastics, but she dared not show herself, and returned to Athens as secretly as she had come.

A few days later, the great feast of the Pan-Athenian procession took place, and Hippolytus, Phaedra and Theseus found themselves in Athens once more. Throughout the festival, Phaedra felt her heart beating wildly, for the young man was standing close beside her. When the ceremonies were over, she hurried straight up to the palace, hoping that there she might find some peace of mind, but as soon as she reached the terrace, she found her eyes sweeping the crowd for a glimpse of the fair young man.

While she was watching, a splendid black horse was led forward. It was unbroken, and no-one had yet succeeded in mounting its back. With brilliant skill, Hippolytus seized the horse by its halter and bounded athwart its flanks. The creature responded to its rider's will instantly and reared upwards superbly upon its hind legs, whilst all the onlookers marvelled at the handsome and courageous young man who had tamed the proud stallion.

With bated breath Phaedra followed the scene from the palace walls, and when everything was over and she found Hippolytus alone, she decided that she must unburden herself once and for all.

"Stay in Athens, Hippolytus," she begged him. "I don't want Theseus any longer. It was he who abandoned my sister Ariadne on Naxos. It was because of him that your mother was killed. He may even kill me. You must take revenge, Hippolytus. The goddess Aphrodite is on our side. Become king of Athens, and I will be your devoted wife and queen."

How little Phaedra knew of Hippolytus! How could such a sick idea find a place in a heart as pure as his? Betray his father, the renowned hero Theseus, whom even the gods admired for his brave and noble deeds? Betray Artemis, the eagle-eyed huntress to whom he had dedicated his life? As if he could perform such a deed!

Hippolytus fixed Phaedra with a gaze of such cold contempt that her heart quailed. And then he hurled the words in her face: "Never! Shame on you!"

With a strangled cry of despair, Phaedra buried her face in her hands and ran to hide herself in the next room, whilst Hippolytus stood thinking only of his father and pitying him with all the power of his soul.

"Great Zeus," he swore at last, "I give my oath that I shall never tell my father what I know. Let her see for herself the injury she was ready to do him."

Phaedra realised, of course, what a terrible thing she had done, but she lacked the will to undo the harm. The one evil deed pushed her on to another, three times more terrible.

"Never! Shame on you!" She echoed his stinging words; "But if I am lost, then you shall be dragged down with me!" Then she tore her clothes, dug her nails into her arms and neck, threw her hair into disorder and burst from the room.

"Help, help!" she cried, and in broken phrases, punctuated by sobs, she laid the blame on the innocent youth. She then shut herself in her room once more and wrote a letter to Theseus, treacherously accusing Hippolytus of the crime she had herself committed. Then, pinning the note to her robe, she hanged herself from the crossbeam of the door and brought her life to a miserable close.

The frightful news soon reached Theseus. When he saw

his wife's body and read the letter, he stood as if transfixed. He could not bring himself to believe the sight before him and the words he read. Yet his wife was dead and how else but through the treacherous lust of his son Hippolytus?

"How could I have been so blind," he cried. "Turn him out and let him never again set foot in Athens!"

At that moment, Hippolytus appeared. "You are making a terrible mistake, father," he said, "I am not guilty."

"You hypocrite! You swore a vow of chastity to the goddess Artemis and now you betray her, your father and your step-mother. It was you who killed her, murderer! Get out! Get out and never set eyes on me again!"

Hippolytus did not wish to speak out, for he had sworn never to lay the blame on Phaedra. For this reason, he decided to swear a solemn oath.

"Listen, father. I swear to Zeus that I will disappear without name or glory, without motherland and without home, pursued by gods and men, if I am evil; and when I die, may my body lie unburied, my bones picked clean by birds of prey. I can say no more."

"Oh, ye gods, what a shameless liar. There's the body, there's the letter. Everything betrays you, ungrateful beast. Leave! I cannot bear the sight of you!"

And rather than reveal the truth, Hippolytus chose to leave. He ran straight to his horses, harnessed them to the chariot, and seizing the reins galloped off down the road towards the Peloponnese.

As soon as he had left, Theseus' anger overflowed: "Oh, father Poseidon, ruler of the seas," he cried, "you promised me three wishes and now I beg for one of them. Do not let Hippolytus reach Troezen."

Why, Theseus, why? Why did you act in haste? Why did you not look more closely? Why did you not turn to others for advice, instead of acting in the heat of the moment? Blinded by your wrath, you took the rash decision and hurled the curse which brought death upon your son!

And as for you, unlucky Hippolytus, your fate is sealed. You will never again ride victorious into Troezen, and the longing maidens will set eyes on you no more. You will never again run at Artemis' side in the cool meadows, and never so much as offer another rose to the goddess you adored, for now death lies in wait for you upon your road!

Unaware of the fate which awaited him, Hippolytus was now skirting the Scironian Rocks, speeding along the rough and narrow road that leads to Corinth between the mountain and the sea. Though his heart was bursting with grief, he guided his chariot with a sure hand over the winding, rock-strewn way. Then, all of a sudden, a huge wave disgorged upon the shore a monstrous bull which bellowed hideously and snorted water from its nostrils. The startled horses bolted and dragged the chariot toward the cliff's edge. Had anyone but Hippolytus been at the reins, they would have tumbled headlong to the rocky shore below. But there was not a charioteer in the world who could match Hippolytus. Heaving upon the reins, he arched his body back like an oarsman and achieved the impossible feat of forcing the bolting horses back upon the road. Pursued by the roaring bull, the horses dragged the chariot along at breakneck speed. Yet Hippolytus held them on their course, avoiding death by a hairsbreadth at every instant. In no time they had left the Scironian Rocks behind them and were galloping madly towards the Isthmus of Corinth with the bull still in pursuit. And here the end came. Although Poseidon's monster had failed to dash Hippolytus against the rocks, an old, gnarled olive-tree proved the final cause of his disaster. A harness-belt streaming in the wind caught on a dry branch and in a second all was over. The horses were hurled into the air, the sturdy chariot was dashed to pieces against the boulders and Hippolytus, tangled in the reins, was dashed over the stones and wounded mortally. As he lay dying, the goddess Artemis appeared upon her chariot, bringing with her his father, Theseus. With an aching heart, the goddess revealed the whole story to the king of Athens, who now knelt weeping at his son's side.

Then the noble youth gathered what strength was left to him, raised his head a little and said: "Do not cry, father, it was not your fault if you were deceived. I shall love you, even from the underworld."

And those were his last words.

When he died, Artemis took the youth and buried him in that same grove at Troezen where he had first set eyes upon the goddess and begun his life-long worship of her.

Heartbroken at the death of his son, and at the great and irreparable wrong he had done him, Theseus came to the sacred grove and marked out the spot where a temple would stand. Soon, a simple but beautiful temple rose at the side of Hippolytus' grave. Here the young man was worshipped as a god, and all the young men and maidens of Troezen brought a lock of their hair before their wedding and offered it to the son of Theseus who had been so unjustly sacrificed. This gesture showed that they would go pure and untouched to their marriage vows.

Thus Hippolytus continued to live on in the memory of the people of Troezen. Indeed, they never admitted that he had died. "How is it possible," they argued, "for Hippolytus to have been killed by his horses? No, the horses didn't kill Hippolytus. He lives. Artemis has taken him up into the sky and placed him among the stars." They showed his grave to no-one. But at night, they would point to a constellation in the sky and say: "There he is." And from that day onwards, the constellation has been called Iniochus, the Charioteer.

...the goddess revealed the whole story to the king of
Athens, who now knelt weeping at his son's side...

Actaeon's cruel fate

And now here is another myth in which a fair young man again suffers an undeserved death. And if in the previous myth we saw that the unjust fate of Hippolytus was the will of the goddess Aphrodite, in this we shall see how Artemis herself behaved cruelly.

From as far back as the age of the fearsome Cronus, a law had existed that any man who set eyes upon a god unless the god himself wished it, must surely die.

It was an unjust law, and one which Artemis applied with unnecessary harshness in the case of Actaeon, who unintentionally chanced to catch sight of the goddess while she was bathing.

It happened on a hot summer's day. Artemis was with a party of nymphs and nereids of the forest. Faint with the heat, they longed to take a bathe to cool themselves. Artemis, however, never bathed in sea or river, lake or spring, because she feared that some indiscreet eye might fall upon her. Up to this moment, indeed, neither god nor man had ever seen the goddess bathing.

So Artemis went with her friends to cool herself in the still waters of a cave, buried high up on the thickly-wooded slopes of Mount Cithaeron. The whole group left their clothes on the rocks and jumped into the crystal-clear waters with happy shouts. Artemis jumped first, and she played and frolicked in the water as if she were a little child. The nymphs and nereids followed her and they all played and laughed together, happy and carefree.

At the same time, a party of hunters happened to be passing by. Among them was Actaeon, the handsome crown prince of Thebes. He had gone on ahead of the others, and, as he was thirsty, was looking for water. Suddenly, he saw the entrance to a cave.

It was the cave where Artemis was. Leaving his dogs outside, the prince went in to look for water. After he had gone forward a few steps, he heard the sound of splashing, and paused thoughtfully.

"No, Actaeon, don't go on," a voice inside him seemed to say. "Remember the law of Cronus. Who knows who may be in the cave?"

Yet Actaeon did go on, and suddenly, rounding a bend in the rock, he came face to face with the party of goddesses.

At that moment, the lovely Artemis was rising from the water. Her lithe body glowed in the half-light of the cave with an indescribable, divine beauty which no man's eyes had ever yet beheld.

It was two nymphs who first saw Actaeon, and a cry of alarm escaped them. Artemis turned to see what had happened and saw Actaeon standing a little further off. She blushed from head to foot in her shame and rage and became more lovely still. The nymphs rushed to shield her from Actaeon's eyes, but the harm had been done. Artemis was so outraged that Actaeon's doom was sealed. The goddess transformed the hapless youth into a deer.

Now a deer, Actaeon ran to escape, but when he emerged from the cave, his own dogs began to hunt him down. Actaeon struggled to speak, to tell his dogs not to harm him, to let them know that the deer they were hunting was their own beloved master. But he no longer had the power of speech, and they bore down on him and sank their fangs into his throat – and the tragic irony of it was that the dogs then went searching for Actaeon to show him their rich prize.

When the other hunters realised that Actaeon was missing, they too went in search of their friend. In the evening, tired and with all hope lost, they slung the slain deer over the back of a horse and took the road back for Thebes. How could any of them imagine that the deer was Actaeon himself, alone among gods and men to have seen Artemis in her nakedness?

The punishments of Artemis were harsh, and for that reason people were careful to behave as the goddess wished.

At Vravron, in Attica, there was a great festival every five years, which had its origin in the following incident: a tame bear used to wander at liberty in the streets of Athens and all the inhabitants thought of it as a holy animal, protected by Artemis. The Athenians, who loved the beast, fed and took care of it. The bear was the children's best friend. They played with it and teased it without its ever losing its temper or doing any of them any harm.

One day, however, a little girl got so carried away with her teasing that she kicked the bear and pinched it and finally took a stick and started beating the creature wherever she could find a target. Then the animal finally lost its temper, lunged at the girl and squeezed her to death in its grip.

When the little girl's brothers heard the terrible news, without pausing to think, they went and killed the bear – killed, that is, the sacred animal protected by Artemis.

After that, a great misery hung over Athens. A terrible disease struck down the children of Attica.

Then the Athenians sent messengers to seek the advice of the oracle and were told that they must dedicate their daughters to Artemis in the guise of a bear.

This was the beginning of the Vravronia, a beautiful ceremony which took place every five years, when the Athenians dressed all their daughters between five and ten in costumes the colour of bear-skins and walked with them in a long procession to the temple of Artemis at Vravron. There, they sacrificed a she-goat or a calf to the goddess, and the priestesses blessed the 'bear girls' as they were called. They then went off to play, and the little plain of Vravron seemed quite changed from its usual self as it filled with the little 'bear girls' running, jumping and dancing with happy cries over the fresh, green turf.

It was only with a great deal of effort that their parents were able to round them up again so they could set off early, for it was a long walk back to Athens.

HEPHAESTUS

A lame child is born

Let us go back once again to that distant time when the goddess Hera married great Zeus and became queen of the skies. Now she was about to give birth to her first child and her joy was indescribable, for she believed that she would bear a son who would be the pride of Olympus and the apple of his parents' eye.

But instead she bore Hephaestus, a baby so crippled and

ugly that as soon as she set eyes on him she took him by his lame leg and...

The words are hard to say. A mother casting away her own son seems cruel beyond belief, yet once it was not so. It is worth leaving the legend aside for a moment to see how and why a deed, which today seems unreasonable and wicked, once seemed right and natural.

If we leaf through the pages of history we shall see that in ancient Sparta, mothers who gave birth to deformed children had to go and throw them into the terrible abyss of Caiadas on the slopes of Mount Taygetus. Whatever their feelings as mothers, it naturally never crossed their minds that what they were doing was wrong; on the contrary, they believed that they were doing their duty to the state, which needed the finest and strongest soldiers. However, this cruel custom did not come into being overnight. It had existed since long, long before, and Sparta, which was a military state, merely kept up the custom longer.

As we have seen in an earlier chapter of this story, this was a time when men lived and fought like wild beasts in the forest in their struggle to survive. A lot of children were born but very few lived; and those that had the least chance of growing up were those that were born crippled. For this reason it did not seem an evil deed to abandon such children, but rather obedience to the will of the gods.

These were times when man's life was hard. His customs were hard, too, and his myths likewise. Strange myths to us, perhaps, but not to the people of those days. However, let us take up our story once again.

When the goddess Hera saw that she had given birth to such a lame and ugly baby, she felt so angry and insulted that she grasped it by one leg, swung it twice round her head and hurled it over Mount Olympus. Such was her strength that the poor baby soared over land and sea for a day and a night, and on the second day, at dawn, it plunged into the ocean and plummeted down into its bottomless depths. Here, no doubt, the baby would have been drowned and lost for ever – had he not been the immortal Hephaestus, god of fire and the forge!

The sea goddesses Thetis and Eurynome took pity on the little god and cared for him. He was raised in a cave of sapphire blue, and ugly and lame though he was, he also grew up to be hard-working and kind-hearted, and he loved the two goddesses who had saved him and brought him up to manhood.

Hephaestus bends the flames to his will

One might have thought that, having been raised in the blue waters by two such goddesses, Hephaestus would have become a god of the sea. But instead he became the god of quite the opposite element. He became the god of fire.

Hephaestus' love for fire began rather like this: One night, when he came out of the sea, he saw flames shooting from the peaks of the mountains. He had stepped ashore on the island of Lemnos, which in those distant times had many volcanoes. It was night, and Hephaestus was entranced by what he saw. He approached the largest of the volcanoes, admiring it in all its savage majesty. He watched the flames rising to the skies and the molten lava rolling down its sides, and the more he looked, the more thoughtful he became. "Perhaps," he thought, "that same fire might be used to forge useful and attractive things from metal."

"I will try," he said in a determined voice. "This molten lava has shown me the way. It may be difficult, but I will succeed." And he threw himself into the work with enthusiasm.

He tried one way, he tried another; he laboured and sweated, but in the end he achieved what he had set out to do. He built a forge on Lemnos and hammered away at the fire-reddened metal, bathed in sweat.

Every day the lame god worked on, hour after hour. In the beginning the work made him very tired. Little by little, however, he began to stand the strain better. The work made him strong. His shoulders became broad, his chest deep and powerful, the muscles of his arms as hard as steel. There was not a giant or a god on Olympus with arms as strong as the god of fire. Yet his legs were still weak. They could hardly support his heavy, well-muscled body. While other gods had wings on their heels, he hobbled along with a stick.

But Hephaestus did not care; he lived only for his work. Soon, there was not another craftsman in the world to match him. He worked in iron, bronze, gold and silver with wonderful skill and produced real works of art.

The golden throne: a 'gift' for Hera

One day, while he was looking at the marvellous things he had been enabled to make with the help of fire, the worthy craftsman remembered the goddesses who had stood by him during his childhood and decided to do something to please them. So he took gold and silver and gleaming stones and made the loveliest jewellery that had ever been seen. Then he offered them as a gift to Thetis and Eurynome in gratitude for all they had done for him in the past.

At a feast on Olympus, Hephaestus' mother, Hera, saw Thetis wearing one of these pieces of jewellery, a necklace which shone brighter than fire itself.

"What lovely jewellery!" exclaimed Hera, when Thetis approached to offer her greetings. "If there is such a marvellous artist in the world, how is it that I have not heard of him? Surely, dear sea-goddess, you will not mind telling me his name?"

Now Thetis could not go against the wishes of the great lady of Olympus and so she was obliged to tell her that it was Hephaestus and that he had given her many other pieces, too, as lovely and lovelier still.

"I think you know Hephaestus," Thetis concluded with a somewhat mocking smile. "Go to him. I'm sure he'd be only too happy to make you some jewels, as well."

And at the very moment when Hera was asking herself whether she should go or not, on distant Lemnos Hephaestus remembered the mother who had cast him from Olympus, and decided to prepare a surprise for her, too. The god's eye sparkled wickedly at the thought that came into his mind, and he threw himself into the task without delay. The bellows swelled the flames of the forge, metals glowed red-hot, the hammer clanged upon the anvil, scattering blinding sparks, while the bare chest of the labouring god gleamed with sweat in the light of the fire.

The muscles rippled in his mighty arms as he worked tirelessly on, bending the heat-softened metal to his will. Hephaestus laboured for hour after hour until at last there stood glowing in the half darkness of the forge a noble throne of solid gold, adorned with gleaming precious stones. The god of fire surveyed his work with pride. The world had never seen a throne like this!

The throne seemed ready – but Hephaestus had not yet

completed his task. He puffed the flames into life once more with the bellows, and then, with a crafty look in his eyes, he took a great pair of tongs, thrust them into the fire and heaved them out again as if they were gripping something heavy, which he flung down on the anvil. Nothing, however, could be seen. Then he took up his heaviest hammer and began to rain ringing blows upon the anvil as if beating something invisible into shape. In fact, that is exactly what Hephaestus was doing – working an unknown metal, invisible to all eyes but his.

With this metal he wrought unbreakable chains which he alone could see; and when he had finished, he bound the chains to the golden throne and sent it as a present to his mother.

As soon as Hera set eyes on the magnificent gift, she leapt to her feet in delight; for she could see only the majestic throne, and not even the faintest outline of the invisible chains. With proud step she advanced and seated herself upon this throne which seemed so fitting for the queen of gods and men.

Alas! She had hardly sat down upon it when the invisible chains closed around her and bound her tightly.

Never before had such cries been heard on Olympus. Immediately, the gods came running, but they couldn't understand what was happening.

"Curse this throne!" shouted Hera.

"Well, get up if you don't like it," Zeus replied.

"Break the chains!" shrieked Hera.

"Which chains?" the gods enquired.

"The ones that have bound me to the throne!"

"She's out of her mind," said Zeus.

"But can't you see that I'm tied?" asked Hera desperately.

"We can't see anything," came the reply.

"Look what a son I bore!" screamed Hera. "Not only lame and ugly, but disrespectful and cruel to his own mother!"

"Come now, you didn't treat him any better yourself," replied Zeus. "Give me your hand and let's get this over with."

"What hand? Can't you see what the villain's done to me?"

Zeus then tried to catch hold of her hand, but came up against something hard. Feeling its outline with his fingers, he realised that Hera was indeed bound with invisible chains to the throne.

"This is more difficult than I thought," said Zeus. "Don't just stand there watching, you others! Come over here and let's see how we can set her free."

First they all tried together, then each one tried on his own. In the end Ares tried with his fearsome weapons; but he only succeeded in terrifying Hera, and had to be dragged away from the throne by force. The queen of the gods was tightly bound to the throne with invisible but unbreakable chains, and nobody could set her free.

"Listen to me," said Zeus then. "Hephaestus chained her up, and he can set her free. The god of fire must come here, and I think Hermes is the most suitable one to bring him to us."

Immensely proud that Zeus placed such confidence in his abilities, the crafty Hermes slipped on his winged sandals and reached Lemnos as quick as lightning. But it was a wasted journey. Though he used all his wiles to persuade Hephaestus to release his mother, or at least come back to Olympus with him, his words fell on deaf ears. Hephaestus just went on hammering away at his anvil without paying any attention, and the messenger of the gods had to come back on his own.

When the other gods saw him returning empty-handed they were seized with despair.

"You can't bring Hephaestus back with cunning words and promises!" shouted Ares, the god of war, springing to his feet. "I know what he needs: brute force and violence. Just you wait here, and I'll bring him back bound hand and foot!"

He quickly strapped himself into his heavy armour, put on his helmet, picked up his weapons, and quick as a flash had reached the forge of Hephaestus.

He burst in and found Hephaestus labouring at his anvil, bathed in sweat.

"Off to Olympus this instant and set your mother free!" snarled Ares in a savage voice. "And I'll take you there in chains if you won't come by yourself!"

These words were hardly out of Ares' mouth when Hephaestus snatched up a blazing log and dealt him a stunning blow on the head, sending sparks flying in all directions. Scared out of his wits, the god of war took to his heels and returned to Olympus scarlet with shame.

Then Dionysus spoke. "I'll bring him to you as quiet as a lamb," said the god of wine calmly.

"Load up the wine, and off we go!" he ordered his followers. Straight away, the satyrs and the maenads sprang to their feet. Dionysus' tutor, pot-bellied old Silenus, untied his donkey and they loaded it up with flasks of wine. Travelling from cloud to cloud, they soon reached the forge of Hephaestus; and when they reached its doors, the song and dance began.

Bathed in sweat, the blacksmith of the gods was hammering away at his anvil as usual when he heard happy voices and songs. He put down his hammer, wiped the perspiration from his brow and went out to see what was happening. When he saw Dionysus and his followers in such high spirits, he burst out laughing.

The god of wine gave him a welcoming slap on the back and immediately raised a cup of cool, sweet wine to his lips. Hephaestus downed it in one gulp and hobbled into the dance singing.

"Some more wine for our friend Hephaestus!" shouted Dionysus, and all the company immediately filled their cups and ran towards him.

"Have this one on me, have this one on me, old fellow!" each one shouted. Hephaestus didn't want to spoil anyone's mood and besides, he was very thirsty, so he downed one cup after another. And this was a wine better than nectar itself!

The donkey felt a load off its shoulders when the flasks were emptied, but then they heaved Hephaestus up on its back, his stomach distended with wine, and so blind drunk he couldn't even stand on his feet.

"Take me wherever you want. No work today!" said the god of the forge; and singing and dancing, they all took the road for Olympus.

It did not take them long to get there. Hephaestus reeled into the great hall and danced drunkenly with all the gods until he caught sight of his mother chained to the golden throne. Forgetting the harm she had done him, and even who had bound her, he released her immediately and they fell into each other's arms.

Let bygones by bygones! From then onwards the lame god stayed on Olympus, loved his mother and was loved by her in return above all else in the world. Now the golden throne was a real gift to Hera – and as for jewellery, it flowed from his workshop like water.

When Zeus saw that Hera and her son were friends once more, he was so delighted that he decreed that Hephaestus take for his wife the most beautiful woman in the world, the radiant Aphrodite, goddess of love.

Alas! Aphrodite was not for Hephaestus, nor he for her. The goddess of love did not love her lame and ugly husband who spent all his time hammering in the light of the flames, sweaty and streaked with dirt. And so the goddess who spread love among men could not offer the same gift to the hard-working god, and she did not stand by his side as she should have done. For her, happiness lay in the admiration her beauty aroused. For him, it lay in hard work and beautiful creations.

Here was a god indeed! How he could work; and what could his hands not shape? For he was a god of a different kind: a god who felt happy when he was tired.

He set up his forge on Olympus and spent most of his

time there. In the middle of it stood a great anvil. In the corner was a broad hearth with glowing coals. Twenty marvellous bellows which he had made with his own hands blew by themselves and fanned the flames the moment he wished.

The god of fire loved his workshop. It made him happy to see the flames rising and the metal glowing red. He never tired of working at his anvil, and the dull rhythmic beat of his hammer upon the fire-reddened metal seemed to him like the music of the gods.

There seemed no limit to what the god's strong hands could create in that forge! From delicate jewellery of matchless craftsmanship to the imposing palaces of the gods on Olympus, rich gifts were showered from the forge of Hephaestus on gods, demigods and even on mere mortals.

The shield of Achilles

Whatever the god made he carved and adorned with peerless skill. If you wish to understand how he worked, see with what art he decorated the shield of the demigod Achilles when the goddess Thetis asked him to make new armour for her son.

The blacksmith of the gods had never forgotten how

..."I will dazzle the eyes of all of human birth who
set eyes on these arms"...

lovingly the mother of Achilles had tended him in his early years. He immediately lit his fires and threw himself into the task saying, "I will dazzle the eyes of all of human birth who set eyes on these arms."

And having made a strong shield, he sat down and covered it with engraved scenes of every kind you can imagine.

In one part, says Homer, he put the sky, the sea, the tireless sun and the full moon. Then he crowned the sky with stars. He put in the constellation of Orion, the Pleiades, the Hyades and last of all the Great Bear, the only one of them which revolves forever in the same spot, never lost beneath the horizon or sunk in the ocean's deep.

On another part of the shield the Olympian craftsman engraved two wealthy cities. In one of them a wedding was being celebrated with feasting and dancing. Maidens were holding lighted torches and singing. Boys were dancing gracefully. In their midst, musicians were playing, while women stood at the doors of their houses looking on in admiration. Having depicted such a scene of joy and love in one part of the town, in another Hephaestus showed two men quarrelling about a debt before the judges, one seeming to say that he had paid everything, and the other denying that he had ever received a penny. Each was demanding a speedy verdict, claiming that the rightness of his own case was obvious. People stood around, siding now with the one and now with the other and gesturing excitedly. Heralds were blowing their bugles for silence, and within the sacred circle the judges were enthroned on seats of carved marble. The heralds passed the rod from judge to judge and one by one each rose to give his verdict. Two talents of gold lay piled before them, to be taken by the judge who gave the fairest decision.

While these scenes were unfolding themselves in the one town, the other was suffering under the scourge of war. Beneath its walls two armies were locked in battle. Bloodthirsty Ares and Athena the defender could be seen among their ranks. Eris was there, too, drifting from one camp to the other and sowing strife in both. And Moera, goddess of fate, was at work, dragging away a dead body here, abandoning a wounded soldier there, and at times allowing a warrior to pass unscathed through the thick of battle.

Next to this scene of war and destruction the immortal Hephaestus placed peaceful scenes from farming life.

In one, a fertile meadow was being ploughed. Guided by their ploughmen, the yoked oxen turned up the dark soil in straight furrows. At the edge of the field a slim girl stood waiting to offer a cup brimming with wine. And having drunk, the ploughmen pushed the blade deep into the earth once more to drive another furrow, clean and straight to the far edge.

Beyond that lay a fenced-off field of wheat, the ears

hanging heavy on their stalks. Raising their sharp sickles in
steady rhythm, the harvesters cut them down in swathes to
be bound in sheaves by children. Staff in hand, the owner
of the land stood looking on in satisfaction. Further off, in
the shade of an oak tree, the carcass of a great ox was being
readied for the pot while women kneaded enough dough to
provide food in plenty for the workers.

Further down, Hephaestus engraved a vineyard where
heavy black grapes were being harvested. Boys and carefree girls were carrying the ripe fruit in baskets. In their
midst a youth sat playing a lyre and singing, while all
around him joined happily in his sweet song.

Elsewhere, the god depicted two fearsome lions snatching a mighty bull from the midst of the herd. It roared in
vain as they dragged it away. The shepherds urged their
dogs on, but to no avail, for they dared not try their teeth
upon these wild beasts. They ran up close and barked, but
then backed off again.

In another place the great craftsman put in a smiling
valley where sheep grazed peacefully in a meadow. Near
them stood the sheepfolds and the thatched huts of the
shepherds.

Finally the tireless god engraved a group of young men
and maidens dancing hand in hand and beating their feet in
rhythm on the ground. The girls were dressed in long
gowns of fine linen and wore garlands of flowers in their

hair. The boys' short robes had the rich sheen of good
cloth, and golden swords were buckled at their waists. Now
the whole group would whirl in circles, swift as the potter's
wheel, then the boys and the girls would form facing lines
and leap and spin with swift, gay grace. All around them a
crowd looked on in admiration while a singer, splendid as a
god, plucked the strings of his lyre and sang while two fine
young dancers twirled in the centre of the floor.

This, in simple words, is how the great poet Homer de-
scribed the marvellous scenes carved on the shield of the
hero Achilles by the lame but tireless master-craftsman of
the gods.

That is how Hephaestus worked: eager and absorbed in
whatever task he undertook, sparing no effort and no pains.
But when the time came to lay down his tools, he would
quit his anvil, take the bellows from the fire, put his ham-
mers and tongs in a silver box, and, having cleaned up the
whole forge, go and wash himself in a perfumed bath.
Taking up a great sponge, he would wipe clean his neck,
his burly arms and his hairy chest; and then, slipping a
golden cloak over his shoulders, he would reach for his
staff and limp homewards to the great hall of the gods on
Olympus.

Good-hearted fellow that he was, he would fill the
golden goblets with wine and, before tasting it himself,

would offer the scented nectar to each of the gods in turn. They would laugh gently as they watched him hobbling round, his weak legs barely able to support his massive body. But Hephaestus did not always need to perform the task himself: when he was very tired, he would serve the gods with his 'magic' tables. Set in motion by a simple movement, they were so constructed that they would roll right across the hall and then return to their places of their own accord.

It always pleased Hephaestus when he returned from his labours and found the gods of Olympus in good spirits. All too often, however, he would come home and see them quarrelling, and this would make him sad.

"You poor things!" he'd say with a laugh, "If only you'd find some work to do, you'd have no time for squabbling!"

But once, when he found his mother angry with Zeus, he was so saddened that he felt he had to give her some serious advice.

"Mother" he said earnestly, "don't you see how bad it will be for all of us up here if you and Zeus quarrel and the other gods take sides? Our fine food will lose its taste and our sweet wine its bouquet. And so, dear mother, how ever wise you may be, I advise you to bow to the will of Zeus, lest his terrible anger seize him and he overthrow the table of the gods. For Zeus is our all-powerful master and if he wished he could topple us all from our thrones. Go now, dear mother, calm him with soft words and bring peace to Olympus once more." And so saying, he filled a golden chalice with sweet wine and handed it to his mother, who took it with a smile. Hephaestus then poured nectar out for all the gods, beginning from the right. Their faces, saddened by the quarrel, now began to light up with smiles as they watched the wise and kind-hearted Hephaestus limping around the palace. Soon, Apollo took up his lyre and cheerful music filled the great hall. Then the Muses sprang up and threw themselves gaily into the dance. The quarrel of the gods was forgotten and wild merrymaking filled the courts of Olympus.

But if Hephaestus could be kind-hearted, he could also inflict fearsome punishment. Who else could have fought and defeated the river god Xanthus, when he threatened to drown Achilles and his brave companions outside Troy?

It was Hera who warned Hephaestus of the danger to the hero, for she knew her son shared her great love for Achilles.

At once, Hephaestus laid down his tools, left his anvil and hurried to Troy. There, armed with his magic fire, he launched his attack upon the river Xanthus.

It was a fearsome battle between fire and water. A whole mighty river was rearing menacingly to drown Achilles and his army, when Hephaestus shot his flaming darts straight at it. The moment he did so, huge flames shot up from both banks of the Xanthus.

Reeds, brushwood and oleander bushes were transformed into flaming torches. Towering flames leapt from
the myrtles, the plane trees and the willows which lined the
river's banks. Fish and eels writhed in the water, choked by
the burning breath of the god, seeking shelter where the
whirling currents had carved the deepest pools. The river
could not bear the torturing flames and begged the god to
stop.

"I will harm Achilles and the Greeks no longer, if only
you will let my waters flow in peace!" Xanthus pleaded.

But instead of this, Hephaestus fanned the flames and
directed them onto the river itself. There was a great hiss of
steam and the waters bubbled like a cauldron on a roaring
log fire. Now the end was near. The waters of the river
were drying up quickly, spitting and spluttering like the
scorching fat of a pig roasted over the coals. Soon it was all
over. The Xanthus flowed no longer, tamed by the burning
breath of the god of fire.

Such was Hephaestus: as strong as fire, as soft as molten
iron and kind-hearted, like every man who loves his work,
mortal or immortal.

Men loved Hephaestus, for of all the gods he seemed the
closest to themselves, and more of a man than a god. Lame,
ugly, neglected in his childhood, yet loving what was
beautiful and difficult, he laboured not like a god but like a

man to achieve his ends.

Hephaestus became a model for all right-thinking and hard-working men. In Athens, where there were many workshops, the Olympian blacksmith was especially honoured and worshipped. Among the great festivals of the city was the Hephaestia, which took place every five years. One of its events was a race in which apprentices competed, holding lighted torches. The Athenians believed that the god helped these young men to become fine craftsmen.

The citizens of Athens even built a splendid temple in honour of Hephaestus. This temple, known today as the Theseion, is the only one in the whole of Greece to have survived the passage of the years unharmed. It is as if fate had a hand in proving that, of all temples, the one devoted to the master craftsman was the most soundly built of all.

On Lemnos, the island where the great blacksmith had set up his first forge, Hephaestus was especially worshipped as the god of fire. The people of the island had a delightful custom connected with this: every year they would put out all the fires in their hearths for a period of nine days; and on the ninth day a ship would bring fresh fire from Delos, the holy island of the Cyclades, and its flames would be carried by torches to every house and workshop on the island. There was a noble motive behind this custom: when the islanders put out their fires, they had to extinguish all ill-feeling, too, and settle all their differences, inspired by the example of the life of Hephaestus. By the time the fresh fires were lit, the people of Lemnos were supposed to be on good terms with one another and ready to start life afresh.

Hephaestus was a wonderful god, however ugly he may have been to look at!

ARES

A handsome villain

Ares was a handsome, well-muscled god, and his shining armour lent added glory to his appearance. That, however, is the only good word one can say for him. When we try to make a list of all there is to admire in this god, we find there is nothing else at all. Perhaps this is because we hate war and Ares was the god of war – the god who loved war, who lived for war and fought hard to bring death and destruction upon us all.

Do you imagine that we are the only ones who do not love this bloodthirsty figure? No! He was never loved.

How wonderfully clearly they depicted his character, those myth-makers of old: evil, pitiless and savage, yet stupid and ridiculous, and by no means the hero he liked to make himself out. Battles, death and blood were his only pleasures. It was of no concern to him who was fighting for a just cause and who for an unjust. It was all the same to Ares as long as fine young men were slaughtered, cities burned to ashes, and whole populations wiped out. His symbols were the spear and the vulture: the spear that slays, and the vulture which feeds on the flesh of the slain.

Ares was helped in his unholy task by Phobus and Deimus, his two sons, whose names meant fear and terror, and by Eris, the goddess who bred hate and conflict. All three followed Ares' orders with zeal and fanned the flames of battle to the highest pitch of murderous destruction. As soon as fighting broke out, Ares would charge, teeth bared, into the thick of battle and cut down every warrior who crossed his path.

His happiness in times of war was matched only by his sufferings when there was peace. If things remained calm for too long, he would hasten in search of the goddess Eris.

"I can't bear this peace!" he would shout. "Why are you sitting there gaping at me? Don't you know your job? Off with you this minute and set men at one another's throats, so that war may break out again and delight us with killing and blood and the groans of the wounded!"

Whenever a battle ended with the dead strewn thick upon the ground, Ares would return to Olympus feeling highly satisfied. Strutting proudly up and down, he would boast of his feats in a thunderous voice, not realising that the other gods had no wish to hear his tales. However, he did have one admirer. This was Aphrodite, the goddess of beauty and love. For, you see, then as now, there were those who were dazzled by a manly figure and suit of shining armour.

Ares and Athena

However, Ares did not always return from battle so pleased with himself, for he was often beaten, and, worse still, made to look a complete fool.

On such occasions he would ask for his father's help, for Ares was the son of mighty Zeus and Hera. Yet he was such an unpleasant character that not even his parents loved him — and they showed it in a thousand ways.

"Almighty Zeus," said Ares' mother one day to the ruler of gods and men, "if I saw to it that Ares was dragged ingloriously from the battlefield with a gaping wound, would you be angry with me?"

"On the contrary," replied Zeus, "I would be delighted. Choose Athena to do the job. She knows how to make him dance like a cat on hot coals!"

This was in the fearful days of the Trojan War, and the
goddess Hera wished to help the Greeks, who were then in
a very difficult situation. The demigod Achilles, angry with
Agamemnon, the leader of the Greek forces, was refusing
to fight; and Ares, thirsty for blood, now took advantage of
the opportunity and slaughtered the Greeks, although he
had already killed countless
brave warriors when he caught sight of Diomedes, the great
hero of the Greek army. Snarling like a maddened beast,
Ares immediately hurled a bronze javelin at him. The
missile sped through the air, but suddenly, as if caught by a
gust of wind, it went off course and fell wide of its mark. It
was not the wind, however, but the hand of Zeus' beloved
daughter Athena which had caught the javelin and turned it
aside. Warned by Hera, Athena had made all speed for the
field of battle; and it was lucky that she did so, for she
saved Diomedes from certain death. Then she rushed to the
hero's side and gave him the courage to strike back at Ares.

Boldly, Diomedes grasped his long spear and charged
straight at the god. Athena guided the point and Diomedes
struck Ares full in the ribs. The god of war let out a roar as
if ten thousand warriors had been wounded at the same
instant, and took to his heels, scared out of his wits. He
soon reached Olympus and ran at once to his father to
complain!

"Serves you right," replied Zeus. "Of all the gods on

Olympus, you're the most hateful. You love nothing but enmity, war and blood. If you weren't my son, I'd have thrown you from Olympus into the depths of Tartarus where you would long forever for a ray of light in the eternal darkness. Now, go and get your wound bound up and try to act a little more sensibly."

Yet how could the god of war act sensibly when he was a born fool?

As soon as his wound was healed, he ran furiously back onto the battlefield searching for Athena.

"I'll teach you, she-dog!" he cried on catching sight of the goddess; and with that he hurled his lance straight at her with brutal force. But Athena jumped nimbly aside and the lance sailed past. With one quick movement she snatched up a great stone, hurled it at Ares and hit him square in the throat.

"Aagh!" A strangled gasp escaped Ares' lips as he tottered and fell headlong, covering seven whole fields with his body. His admirer Aphrodite ran straight to his aid, but the daughter of Zeus immediately struck her across the chest with her heavy hand. So hard was the blow that the eyes of the goddess of love clouded over and she, too, fell unconscious at Ares' side. Now the pair of them lay beaten and humiliated in the dust.

"If all who help the Trojans were like you, this war would have ended long ago," said Athena in a mocking voice, leaving them stretched out upon the silent earth.

From then on, whenever Ares caught sight of Athena he hastily took himself off in the opposite direction. But he was not always fast enough. One day, while he was quarrelling with Demeter, the goddess of agriculture, Athena suddenly appeared before him, and before he had time to escape, the haughty goddess dealt him another painful lesson.

As we saw in a previous chapter, Ares had always hated Demeter. He couldn't stomach her opposition to his warlike schemes and so, one day, when he happened to see her standing alone at the gates of Olympus, he ran up to her and cried, "I know you are plotting against me, you and the goddess of peace. You and that Eirene, you're never out of each other's sight – sitting there together teaching men to cultivate the land, making them love work and hate war, and hate me, too. And look what's come of it! They haven't built me one temple worthy of the name in the whole of Greece. Not only that, but instead of dying like men on the field of battle, they now prefer to be carried off by old age, sickness and overwork. Just watch your step, you miserable creature, or I'll..."

But suddenly, glancing round, Ares found Athena standing right beside him! He broke off in mid-sentence and tried to walk away with what dignity he could, but the goddess of wisdom grasped him firmly by the arm.

"Come back here, my little hero," she said and with a sudden quick movement she snatched his helmet from his head and flung it far away. While it was still rolling noisily across the paving stones, Athena grabbed Ares' heavy shield and threw it in the same direction. Then she tore his fearsome lance from his hands and angrily tossed it aside, crying, "Now be off with you, bold warrior, and next time, stay away from those I love and are kind to gods and men."

Utterly humiliated, and blushing to the roots of his hair, Ares bent to pick up his scattered weapons and hastily took himself off, not daring to look the two goddesses in the face.

"And behave yourself on the way!" came the mocking voice of the daughter of Zeus as the god of war fled from her sight.

Ares' son and Heracles

If it had only been Athena who made Ares look such an utter fool, things might not have been too bad for him, but the god of war also suffered a terrible defeat at the hands of the renowned hero Heracles, who both wounded him and killed one of his sons.

Ares had a son of whom he was mightily proud. He was called Cycnus, and he was so strong that nobody could stand up to him. He had even less brains than his father, however, and his heart was harder still. Now this Cycnus took it very hard that his father was the only god who had no temple, and so he decided to build him one himself. To his crude way of thinking, the temple would look more beautiful if it were built of human bones and skulls. The idea appealed to him so much that he threw himself into the task, killing and killing in his quest for building materials until the inhabitants of the whole region, from Tempe to Thermopylae, trembled at the very sound of his name. His murderous search went on until, one day, Heracles happened to pass that way. When Cycnus saw the hero's giant frame, he told himself that here were some fine big bones for his temple, and charged in for the kill. Alas for Cycnus, he had forgotten that Heracles was the invincible son of Zeus. Heracles made short work of Cycnus. His temple remained half-built and he himself passed on into the kingdom of the dead. Mad with rage, Ares burst like a thunderclap from Olympus to take revenge upon his son's killer – but before long he was back again, screaming with pain. Heracles, a foe not to be taken lightly, had pierced Ares with his lance and wounded him horribly. Now the god of war did not want to set eyes upon anybody. He shut himself up alone and wept over the three harsh blows that fate had dealt him: the loss of his son, his wounded body and his wounded pride.

In time, however, the pain of his wound eased and he

forgot his shame. Only his grief for his son was left, and so he decided to build him a memorial. For this purpose he called king Ceyx, the father-in-law of Cycnus, and ordered him to set the inhabitants of the region to work and build an imposing monument. He even commanded them to embellish it with all the bones and skulls which Cycnus had collected. "So much hard work should not go to waste," he thought. "Only thus will the memory of my son's great achievements remain forever fresh in the minds of men."

When the monument was completed, Ares came to see it and found every detail just as he had imagined. "Now it is clear for all to see," he said to himself, "how much worthier than Heracles was my son Cycnus. I am convinced that it was only with the help of Athena that Heracles was able to kill my boy."

While these thoughts were passing through Ares' mind, a low rumbling began to trouble his ear, a rumbling which grew ever louder and more threatening. Some great evil was surely approaching. Ares' courage failed him, and he called out to Zeus with all the strength in his lungs.

"Help, father!" he screamed, but so loud was the noise that it drowned the cries of the terrified god.

The cause of it all was the sacred river Amarus, which was sweeping down from the mountains in a huge, roaring wall of water which no power on earth could check. Golden-haired Apollo had ordered the river god to hurl his foaming torrents upon Cycnus' memorial. The end was not long in coming. Paralysed with fear, Ares did not know which way to turn. At the very last moment, he took off and just managed to gain the safety of a hill-top. From this vantage point he saw disaster strike. In a matter of seconds the rushing waters had carried all before them and out towards the sea.

Soon the land lay bare, washed clean of memorial, bones and skulls. Nothing was left to tell of Cycnus and his bloody deeds but a despairing Ares weeping over his latest defeat.

Caught in the trap

But life cannot be all disappointments, and so, to forget his troubles, Ares sought the company of the lovely Aphrodite. The goddess of love was the only one who saw the war god in a different light. In her eyes, Ares was the mighty god of war chariots, the brave-hearted warlord, defender of cities, in shining armour and golden helmet. To her he was the fearless lancer, protector of kings, upholder of the rule of law and punisher of rebels, the invincible fortress of Olympus.

Of course, nobody else believed all this, perhaps not even Ares himself; but he swelled with pride to think that Aphrodite held such a high opinion of him. In her delightful company the war god forgot all his humiliations and dreamed of mighty deeds of valour. If only they had been content just to see each other! But mere friendship was not enough and the result was a disgrace worse than any that had yet befallen either of them. For Ares chose to ignore the fact that Aphrodite was already married to Hephaestus. Knowing that the goddess of beauty was none too fond of her crippled husband, he persuaded her to spend the night with him — and on Hephaestus' very bed. He had learned that the blacksmith of the gods was about to leave for Lemnos and told himself that here was an opportunity too good to be missed.

Too good to be missed! That was precisely what it turned out to be, though not in the way that Ares had imagined. For a humiliation was in store for the pair of them such as would never be forgotten.

The god Helios had seen them whispering together and overheard every word they said. He could never forgive an act of unfaithfulness, and particularly when it was directed against a god as beloved and good-natured as Hephaestus; and so he ran to warn him.

The blacksmith was outraged when he heard the news, and it was not long before a cunning idea came into his quick mind. Without wasting a moment, he ran to his workshop and forged some invisible nets which he hung from his bedroom ceiling. Then he bid a loud farewell to

everybody, to make it seem as though he were leaving for
Lemnos. All he really did, however, was to go and hide
nearby.

It was not long before Ares and Aphrodite were caught
in the crafty god's trap. They had hardly seated themselves
upon the bed when down came the invisible nets upon their
heads, wrapping them both so tightly in their folds that they
could not move an inch. And worse was to come: a few
moments later the door was flung open and there stood
Hephaestus with all the gods. Roars of mocking laugher
burst from their lips when they beheld the guilty couple

enmeshed in the nets. Scarlet with shame, Ares and Aphrodite dared not look the other gods in the eyes. How unbelievably foolish the pair looked: two great gods of Olympus caught like rats in a trap and not even able to hide their shame while everyone mocked them! Now they were at Hephaestus' mercy and obliged to wait until he saw fit to set them free and put an end to their sufferings. But the god of fire was in no hurry to do any such thing. On the contrary, he added the final touch to their shame by taunting them with contemptuous words while all the gods looked on. In utter despair, Ares struggled to set himself free. He strained with every ounce of his strength to burst his bonds, but the only thing that happened was that his face turned an even brighter shade of scarlet than before. The gods burst into renewed gales of laughter at the sight and one of them said, "Now they're getting what they deserve. Crime doesn't pay! When the hare stops off to browse in other people's gardens, then even the tortoise catches up with him in the end!"

Finally the other gods persuaded Hephaestus to set the guilty couple free. Their heads hanging in shame, they slunk hastily from the accusing gaze of the gods and fled from Olympus. Aphrodite went to hide her shame on distant Cyprus while the god of war ran and concealed himself in Thrace, a remote land swarming with fierce warriors. Ares was never to forget these indignities he had suffered at the hands of Hephaestus, nor the memory of the stunning blow from the blazing log which the blacksmith had once dealt him on Lemnos. There was no denying it: Hephaestus had shown himself to be yet another god for the blustering Ares to be wary of.

Ares disappears

Yet the god of war was tortured by the thought of all his misfortunes. To be the fearsome god of blood-drenched battles, but still the laughing-stock of Olympus? No! These ever more frequent humiliations were more than he could bear, and he hunted for some opportunity to prove himself bold and worthy of his name.

And it was not long before he had found one – or at least he thought he had.

"Now you will see who I am!" he shouted one day to the other gods and he charged forth from the palace like a maddened beast.

The reason for this sudden show of bravery was the appearance of two giants, the sons of Aloeus, who were threatening Olympus and wished to try their strength against the gods.

"Try your strength against me, if you dare!" Ares roared out his challenge to the two Aloades, but before he had time to make the slightest move, one of the giants seized him from behind while the other stuffed a dishcloth in his mouth. Now Ares could neither cry out nor struggle free, and in a flash the two giants had bound him fast and carried him off.

Thirteen months went by, and not only had Ares failed to return but there was no news of him from anywhere. In the meantime, all wars had come to a halt and life had become happy and peaceful.

Unfortunately, however, Zeus was worried by his disappearance. He called Hermes and ordered him to search for Ares.

"After all, he is my son and your brother," he told Hermes, "and then you should not forget that when men cease to suffer, they cease to obey the gods. Look everywhere. He must be found!"

Now, sad to say, Hermes took Zeus exactly at his word and began a tireless hunt for his lost brother. By dint of much searching and asking around he finally tracked down the giants' step-mother and she revealed where Ares was to be found. He was on the island of Naxos, locked up in a bronze prison that was little more than a cage, and so small that the god of war could only fit in bent double. When Hermes set him free, Ares was half dead and could not even stand upright. A long time went by before he was sufficiently recovered to dare show his face on Olympus. As for the two Aloades, they, as we saw in a previous chapter, were defeated by a woman, the goddess Artemis. So once again, the god of war was doubly disgraced.

It is easy enough to put on the airs of a hero, difficult to be one. But when Ares saw the hideous Typhoon swooping down on Olympus with horrible shrieks, he didn't even have time to put on airs. Fear turned his knees to jelly when the frightful monster approached, spreading death and destruction; and while his father Zeus snatched up his thunderbolts and sprang to the attack, the "mighty fortress of Olympus," as he loved to be called, turned himself into a wild boar and rushed panic-stricken towards the furthermost slopes of the mountain. Falling over his own legs in his desperate urge to escape, he soon found himself on the plains below, and from there his fear-driven flight took him northwards into Thrace. He crossed the Hellespont and fled across Asia Minor into Syria without once pausing for breath or even daring to look over his shoulder. And while Zeus was waging a victorious struggle against the hideous Typhoon, a trembling Ares continued his headlong flight until he reached the land of Egypt. There, half dead with fear and utterly worn out, he fell senseless in a ditch. He was a sorry sight indeed: scratched and bleeding, his legs too weak to support him and his whole boar-like body racked by unbearable pains. To such depths had the once majestic god of war now fallen.

Yet even this latest indignity was soon to be forgotten. As soon as it became known that, with the help of Athena and Hermes, Zeus had defeated the Typhoon, and that the monster now lay crushed beneath the huge mass of Mount Etna, our hero took courage and resumed his former shape. Not daring to show his face on Olympus, he once more set about his old task of trying to stir up troubles among the peoples of the earth, believing that the blood they shed in murderous battle would wash away his shame.

For, you see, Ares could not grasp the fact that war itself was the greatest shame on earth and that first he must be washed clean of it, and then the other gods of Olympus, and finally the whole of mankind.

PALLAS ATHENA

The birth of Athena

Athena, goddess of wisdom, was born from the head of Zeus. An unusual birth, but one with a very logical explanation: wisdom springs from the head of the lord of gods and men!

There is a strange myth which tells us how this came about.

In those distant times when Olympian Zeus ruled over the heavens and the earth, a great danger came to threaten the almighty lord of the world.

Nobody had any suspicion of the threat which was looming, not even Zeus himself. However, there was one goddess, Mother Earth, who could even foresee the fates of the immortals. She alone saw the danger and appeared before Zeus, saying:

"It is a terrible burden to bear such fearful tidings, but tell of them I must. Hear me, Zeus, thrower of thunderbolts. You have committed a grave error and an evil fate is in store for you. A son of yours will oust you from your throne, just as befell your father, great Cronus, and your grandfather Uranus before him. You should never have married Metis, daughter of white-haired Oceanus, even though she is the wisest of the immortals and knows better than any of us how to tell good from evil. And now listen to me carefully: you will have two children by this sea-goddess. The first of them will be Athena, who is already in her mother's womb. The new goddess will be as wise and powerful as you are yourself. She will be a good and loving daughter, more willing to help you in your work than any other of the immortals. Later, however, Metis will bear you a son who will surpass in wisdom, strength and daring all the other gods of Olympus, including even you. But he, unlike Athena, will not bow to your rule. Cruel and ambitious, he will use his power to further his own interests. And when that happens, woe betide you, son of Cronus! For you will be cast down from the lofty heights of Olympus into the yawning depths of Tartarus, and exchange your airy palaces for a dungeon dark as pitch. While the new lord of the world is seated upon your stately throne, you will lie groaning in heavy chains with no hope of ever being set free."

"Mother of the gods," replied Zeus, "I can hardly believe the things which you foretell. Indeed, had these words come from any other mouth, I would not have believed them. I know that you speak nothing but the truth. Yet let me tell you this: I shall not bow to my fate; I shall overcome it!"

"That, too, I know," replied the goddess Earth, "and that is why I spoke to you." And with these words she vanished from his sight.

Without a moment's delay Zeus hastened in search of Metis. He told her nothing of what he had learned, but lulled her to sleep with sweet words. And then, so that this dreaded son might never be born, Zeus enfolded the wise Oceanid within his arms and took her into his own body.

By this union Zeus effectively averted his fate, and what is more, by absorbing the wise goddess into his own flesh he acquired the gift of the knowledge of good and evil.

The danger that had threatened Zeus was past, but strange things began to happen within his body, for Metis was about to give birth to his immortal daughter, Athena.

Very soon Zeus began to be afflicted with terrible headaches. In a desperate attempt to relieve the pain, he called for Hephaestus and ordered him to split his head open.

Hesitantly, Hephaestus lifted his great hammer and brought it down with controlled force upon his father's brow and... a miracle occurred!

Immediately, there was a flash of unearthly light and from the head of Zeus sprang Pallas Athena, goddess of wisdom. She was no new-born babe, but a lovely, blue-eyed maiden endowed with wisdom, courage and strength. She wore a long robe and a shining helmet. A heavy shield hung from her left shoulder and in her right hand she clasped a long spear.

With a shout of triumph and a wave of her keen-pointed lance she greeted all the gods and sprang lightly to the ground. As she did so, the whole of creation was overwhelmed with the majesty of her sudden appearance. Olympus shook to its very roots. The earth gave a terrifying shudder, the blue sea was whipped into fury and the sun reined in his immortal horses and stood motionless in the sky.

"Hail to the new goddess, daughter of Zeus!" cried the gods with one voice, so dazzled were they by the triumphal manner of Athena's coming.

Pleased by the warmth of her reception, the goddess of wisdom inclined her head to Zeus and all the gods. Then, as if she found her appearance in some way displeasing, she removed the helmet from her head and unslung the weapons from her divine shoulders.

"May I never need to use them!" she exclaimed and laid them at her father's feet.

Zeus' face lit up with pleasure at his daughter's submissive gesture and the wise words which had accompanied it. Deeply moved, he drew her towards him and embraced her tenderly. From this moment onwards, Pallas Athena was to be his most beloved daughter.

Athena truly had no wish to bear arms, and hated war. Yet often the goddess of wisdom was forced to take up her weapons. Although she had a passionate love of progress, civilisation and the peaceful works of man, when these were threatened, she did not hesitate to fight in their defence.

For this reason alone did the daughter of Zeus sometimes become a goddess of war. And then she was rightly called Athena Nike, the Victorious, for she was invincible. Yet never for a moment did victory make her forget her hatred of war. It is always the same: when the need arises, the first to throw themselves into battle are those who love peace most!

And whenever a war came to an end, Athena would hand her weapons back to Zeus. She never liked to be seen armed for battle, and never boasted of her victories.

The goddess of inventions and the arts

She was indeed a being of rare qualities. One might have thought she would have preferred to be an ordinary person rather than a goddess. She spent most of her time far away from Olympus among the homes, the workshops and the fields of men. And there, in their midst, she watched over them, inspired them and encouraged those who loved beautiful works. With the aid of mortals, or on her own, she sought for ways to lighten the burdens of those who laboured.

It was astonishing how the goddess helped mankind. Her quick brain never rested for a moment. It was forever hard at work and busily thinking.

Thus Athena invented the distaff and the loom and taught women to spin, to weave and to embroider with good taste and skill; and thus she taught men the art of pottery and how to paint beautiful scenes on their vases — and to make their task easier she invented the potter's wheel. To help builders, she invented the plumb-line and, later, the roof-tile. For musicians, she created the flute and the trumpet. She taught housewives how to prepare food and made the first cooking utensils for them. She even showed men how to tame horses, and built the first chariot with her own hands.

Idea after idea flowed from the mind of the tireless goddess, but her greatest gifts to man were the fine arts, writing and the sciences, gifts whose development in ancient Greece were later to surprise the whole world. It is worth dwelling further on this subject, but to do so we should follow the story back to where it really begins.

One day, Athena was seated on a hillside looking out thoughtfully across the valley to where a dozen women were at work in the fields. Standing side by side in a line, they were trying to break the earth with primitive hoes and sow the seed, but hard though they worked it was to little effect.

That is how ploughing was done in those far-off times. Those were the days when men lived in clans, large groups whose members were all united by ties of blood and the eternal need to rely on one another for help. Since the menfolk were away all day hunting in the forests, the leader of the clan was not a man but a woman, a mother-figure chosen as most worthy of the position from amongst all the females in the group. She was called the matriarch or the mother ruler. And it is from this word that that period takes its name. They were difficult years, with much work, many dangers and little to eat; and what there was had to be shared out equally and with great care so that the whole clan might survive.

The goddess Athena knew of all this, and now, as she looked down upon the toiling women, she wondered how she might help them. Suddenly her glance fell upon two oxen peacefully cropping the fresh green grass and her eyes lit up with joy. She had thought up a new invention – the plough.

"From now on, beasts shall plough the fields," she said to herself. "With just one man to guide them, the work can be done much better than by all these women together. If the men can come back out of the forests and take up farming and raise animals, then maybe life will become less hard for the human race." Who could have known, however, what the final consequences of this invention were to be?

At first, all went well and Athena was delighted. Now mankind had more food: food to spare, in fact. Within the clans, leadership now passed to the menfolk. However, it was not this which worried Athena, but something else.

Now that more was being produced, a part of the population stopped working and began to live off the fruits of the others' labours. Worse still, those who did not work got richer, whilst those who did work found themselves without even the bare necessities. To her dismay, Athena saw human society dividing into two classes: masters and slaves.

Athena was appalled by what had taken place. Goddess of wisdom she might be, but she could never have foreseen that this would happen. Yet that is the way of the world.

When a new discovery is made, nobody, not even the gods themselves, can foretell the changes it may bring to men's lives. And thus it was with the plough, that simple tool drawn by beasts: to some it brought a life of ease, and to others only misery. Faced by this problem, what could Athena do now? Worst of all, what could she do when her father Zeus actually preferred this new order of things?

"Why, not even all the gods are free," he said. "Aren't the Titans imprisoned in Tartarus? Isn't Prometheus chained to a mountain in the Caucasus? Or perhaps," added the lord of the world, "you think that men deserve to live better than the gods?"

These words brought no comfort to the goddess of logic. As long as she saw strong and able men merely sitting idle she could find no peace. She racked her brains for a solution until suddenly the vision of a dazzling new world flashed before her eyes. In the mind of Pallas Athena three great concepts had been born: fine arts, the written word and science. The goddess of wisdom had found the great role for which she was destined. Now to work!

And joyful work it was, as exhilarating as a dance, as inspiring as a song. Tirelessly the goddess laboured, led forward by her keen mind, and helped by her quick hands until she had schooled mankind in the fine arts of sculpture, architecture and painting, which have ever since been known as the arts of Athena. Together with her sisters, the nine Muses, she taught men to love poetry, dancing and music and quickened their spirits so that they would be moved by beauty and true art.

And so the miracle took place. Grace, harmony and the love of all things beautiful came into the world.

Life changed beyond recognition. Ugliness gave way to beauty. The cities blossomed with temples, monuments and innumerable statues, lovely beyond belief. Their very number and their surpassing beauty give some measure of the loving care which was lavished upon them. Thousands of years have passed since then, and yet the skill of the hands which formed them still shines from creations which even now dazzle the world with their perfection.

And thus, with the advent of creative work, savagery waned, to be replaced by a more humane approach to life. Indeed, without such an approach no great art can flourish.

The same is equally true of all real science – and there was no science which Pallas Athena did not teach mankind. She gave them mathematics, astronomy and medicine. For her services in the last of these fields she was called Athena Hygeia.

The daughter of Zeus even taught men how to build ships, and by this means civilisation was carried to the ends of the earth to show how the love of beauty can sweeten life.

But what about the slaves?

Unfortunately, the slaves remained slaves. Thanks to their labours, free men could occupy themselves with the arts, science and letters, yet the slaves themselves could not enjoy the beauties of the world.

In spite of this, the life of the slave in ancient Greece was not always miserable, for the Greeks were an artistic people who lived simply themselves and were not cruel by nature.

But as the centuries passed, so the situation worsened. Rome conquered Greece and grew into a mighty empire where the love of beauty slowly gave way to a love of wealth. Art declined into a commercial activity. Very few now worked solely with the idea of creating something beautiful. A man's worth was no longer judged by what he had done, but by what he possessed. Noble feelings faded from the hearts of free men, and in their relentless pursuit of wealth they declined once more into mere barbarity.

When this happened the life of their slaves became intolerable, for they were no longer even considered human. So degraded had the tastes of the citizens of Rome become that they set slaves to fight one another to the death merely to provide their masters with amusement. To house such "entertainments" they built huge amphitheatres, called circuses, where thousands of onlookers could enjoy the spectacle of innocent victims being slaughtered by others of their own kind.

But not all these slaves bowed meekly to their fate. One of the gladiators, Spartacus, led a brave uprising which shook the cruel might of Rome to its very foundations. He died on the field of battle, fighting for the liberty of his fellow slaves. This happened 71 years before the birth of Christ.

That, in brief, was the lot of the luckless slaves. But now let us leave that age where the gods had become lifeless statues, and return once more to the mythical times when the immortals were still powerful and active and often shared the joys and sorrows of common men.

Here we shall find our beloved goddess once more, fighting at the side of those who preferred kindness and beauty to hoards of wealth.

In those days, too, times could be hard. Time and again some barbarous enemy would threaten to wipe all beauty from the face of the earth. Yet the goddess of wisdom would always know what had to be done. Leaving her peaceful work aside, she would run for her weapons; and, having armed herself, she became another goddess altogether – a creature of iron will, terrible to behold. She would buckle on a fearsome breastplate wreathed with snakes, in the centre of which was a horrible Gorgon's head which turned all enemies to stone. She would quickly slip on her fighting helmet and seize her heavy shield and long spear and then she would surge forward into battle, to

...for hearth and home, for the lives of their
helpless wives and children...

protect the heroes, to join the warrior's ranks and give them courage as they fought for hearth and home, for the lives of their helpless wives and children and for the very future of the world.

One of Athena's greatest enemies was Ares, the bloodthirsty god of war, but an even more dangerous foe was Eris, the goddess who sowed the seeds of hatred.

She had little to fear from the former, for Ares dreaded the thought of crossing her path on the field of battle, knowing that whenever he did so she would teach him to his cost that wars are not won by brute force but by intelligence and the ideals of freedom. We have seen in a previous chapter what humiliating defeats Ares suffered at the hands of Athena.

But how was the goddess of war to fight Eris, who worked in secret and was as slippery as an eel? She needed no more than a single crack in the defences to steal in and strike at the defenders with her cunning weapons and sow hatred in their ranks.

Whenever this happened, all was lost. For all Athena's efforts, certain ruin would follow. Every warrior knew this, just as he knew that the goddess' power to help was dependent on the will of mortals to succeed. There was even a saying about it: "To Athena's efforts you must add your own."

When the people faced the threat of destruction with a

united front, Athena was there to defend their cause, struggling to save lives and bring peace after a speedy victory. The battle done, there would come the task of building anew from the ruins even more beautifully than before. Here, too, Athena would be in the forefront as Athena Ergani, goddess of toil.

Arachne provokes Athena

Yet from time to time Athena wished to be alone – not to rest, but to work at her loom. Then for endless hours she would forget her cares, weaving and embroidering – for Ergani is above all the goddess of household crafts.

Robes woven with matchless skill graced the figures of the gods. They were all the work of the tireless goddess, who offered her masterpieces not only to the immortals but to heroes and common men as well. Their wives loved the art of Zeus' daughter and many of them wove and embroidered as the goddess had taught them. Yet no woman in her right mind ever considered that her skills might be compared with Athena's.

Far away in the kingdom of Lydia, however, lived a princess who could weave and sew so well that her skill really did approach that of the goddess. Her name was Arachne and she wove threads as fine as gossamer into fabrics that were eagerly sought after by princesses and noblewomen the world over.

Unfortunately, Arachne fell prey to that sickness which afflicts all too many gifted people. She became swollen with pride and scorn and spoke slightingly of all other weavers, regardless of the quality of their work. She even reached the stage where she told a group of ladies who had come to admire her creations: "Why, I am even better than Athena. I can more than hold my own against her skill!"

Now among the visitors was an old woman whom nobody recognised. When Arachne had said her piece, this old woman stepped forward and replied:

"Let me give you a piece of advice, my girl. The years may have bowed my shoulders but they have also taught me many things, so pay heed to what I say. Pit your skills against any mortal you wish, but not against a goddess! And now beg Pallas Athena to forgive you for what you have just said."

"Age has softened your brain, old woman!" came Arachne's scornful retort. "Keep your advice for your daughters, not for me. Athena knows she would be beaten and that is why she dare not show her face here!"

"Yet here I am, Arachne. Let us compare our skills!" cried the stranger in a resonant voice. And immediately a dazzling radiance enveloped the old woman and transformed her into her true shape. It was Pallas Athena herself, daughter of Zeus!

...For endless hours she would forget her cares, weaving
and embroidering...

All those present went down on their knees before the goddess – except Arachne, who remained proudly upright, eager to accept the challenge, quite unsuspecting of the fate which was about to overtake her.

The test of skill began. Athena seated herself at the loom. Her divine hands tossed the shuttle with swift, flowing movements. As if dancing to the rhythm of some heavenly melody, her fingers flickered amongst the coloured bobbins, drawing each thread into its correct position.

The goddess had finished. Before her, woven with matchless skill, lay the Acropolis of Athens. All the gods of Olympus were gathered there to decide into whose protection the city of Cecrops should be delivered – Athena's or Poseidon's. In one corner, the gods were seen punishing mortals for their evil deeds. The whole scene was set off by a border of olive leaves.

On her loom, Arachne had woven a scene showing the gods carried away by their own weaknesses and low instincts. Every detail of the tapestry was an insult to the gods of Olympus. Uncontrollable anger raged through the virgin goddess when she set eyes upon it, yet she could find no fault with Arachne's craftsmanship. The work was indeed perfect – as perfect as her own.

"A pity," remarked the goddess, "but let this be a lesson to those who have not learned that art springs not from insolence but love!" and with these words she seized the tapestry with its insulting pictures of the gods and tore it into shreds.

As the pieces fluttered to the floor, so Arachne plunged from the heights of pride into the lowest depths of humiliation. The shame was more than she could bear. Picking up a rope, she knotted one end into a noose and hanged herself. But Athena reached her before it was too late, and prising the knot loose, she said:

"Live and go on weaving as you are now, hanging from this rope: you and all your descendants, you swollen-headed creature!" And with these words she transformed her into a spider, an insect whose name in Greek is the very same as that of the proud princess.

Ever since, Arachne has hung suspended from a thread, weaving with ceaseless perfection, as she did in the days when she was a human being. But now, as then, there is no love in her work, and nobody calls it a work of art. And so, whoever sees a spider's web brushes it aside.

The soothsayer Teiresias

If Athena was strict with others she was equally severe with herself. Loving nothing but fine workmanship and true craftsmen she denied herself every other pleasure. For this reason she never fell in love, never married, and remained for ever a virgin goddess.

Thus she was doubly insulted when once a man caught sight of her while she was bathing, although the poor fellow had never intended to intrude. Scarlet with shame and humiliation the goddess immediately sealed the man's eyes. After that, they never opened again: he was blind. Yet when the goddess saw him sightless and stumbling she at once took pity on him and wished to give him back his eyesight. But, alas, this was no longer possible. And so, to right the wrong which she had done him, the goddess sharpened his hearing so that he could understand the language of the birds and see into the future. Athena also gave him a rod with the magic power of guiding his foot-steps as surely as if he could see. The name of this blind man was Teiresias and he became the greatest soothsayer in all mythology.

This myth shows us how the goddess' severity could turn to lenience and goodwill. Indeed, the spirit of mercy which moved Athena was so widely recognised that wher-ever a law court could not decide whether the accused was guilty or innocent, because the judges were equally divided in their opinion, then the accused was set free. In such cases the final vote was Athena's, and she always cast it in favour of the person standing trial. It is said that the daughter of Zeus acquired this right because she founded the Areos Pagos, the highest court of Athens.

The city of Pallas Athena

Athena's great virtues and her services to mankind caused her to be worshipped throughout Greece. In every city, Athena the Protector was honoured and a small wooden statue of her, the Palladium, was carefully guarded; for if it were lost or stolen, the city, too, would be lost – or so they believed.

Athena's favourite city, however, was the one that bore her name – Athens. The Athenians regarded her as their most important goddess and it was to her that the Acropolis and almost all the temples on it were dedicated.

The goddess worked tirelessly for the city. She helped Cecrops, the city's founder and its first king, to fortify the Acropolis and to raise lovely buildings on its summit.

Zeus' daughter also brought up Erechtheus, who succeeded Cecrops as king of Athens. There is even a myth which says that Erechtheus was the son of Athena and Hephaestus; but the Athenians, who wanted their goddess to be a virgin, never accepted this story.

"No," they said, "Athena has always been a maiden and Erechtheus is the son of Hephaestus and mother Earth." And to strengthen their argument they called him Erichthonius, meaning "he who came from the earth".

According to the Athenians, the Earth did not wish to bring up Erechtheus after she had given birth to him. And so she went in search of Athena, and having found her, laid the baby at her feet, saying:

"This baby belongs to you. It was you Hephaestus wanted for his wife, not me, so you bring up the child. Here, take it and look after it yourself."

Athena looked down with pity on the new-born babe which stretched out its arms to her.

"Yes, I shall raise it," said the daughter of Zeus; and with these words she took the child, put it in a basket and rocked it to sleep. At its side she placed a sacred snake to protect it from danger, and when she had covered it so that nothing could be seen, she took the basket to Aglauros, one of the three daughters of King Cecrops, and gave it to her, saying:

"Look after this basket for me. Tell no one that I gave it to you, and whatever you do, do not open it – for if you do, great harm may befall you."

The goddess, you see, did not want anyone to know that she would have to bring up another woman's child.

"I will come back for the basket before night falls," added Athena, and without further delay she hastened away, anxious to complete the task of fortifying the Acropolis of Athens.

As soon as Athena had left, the curiosity of Aglauros began to get the better of her. Disregarding the goddess' warning she went and opened the basket.

Immediately she did so, the snake shot out from beneath the coverings and reared threateningly. The mere sight of it was enough to drive Cecrops' daughter wild with terror. In her panic, she ran blindly away and fell headlong from the Acropolis to meet her death on the rocks below.

A passing crow bore the news to Athena, who at that moment was bringing a huge rock to reinforce the walls of the Acropolis. When she heard, the goddess dropped the rock in horror and ran to find the child. Taking it in her arms, she carried it off to her temple and there raised it as her own.

And ever since, the huge mass of stone which Athena had been carrying has remained exactly where she let it fall. It is called Lycabettus hill and it rises from the very centre of present-day Athens. As for the crow which brought the dreadful news, the goddess changed its colour. Until then, crows had been beautiful white birds and favourites of the goddess, but from that day on they became an inky black and their voices changed to a mournful croak. The daughter of Zeus could no longer bear the sight of them and forbade them ever again to approach the Acropolis.

From then on the owl replaced the crow in Athena's affections, and its great shining eyes symbolise wisdom and deep thought.

When Erechtheus became king of Athens, he beautified

and improved the city. With the help of Athena he built the
first horse-chariot, discovered how to refine silver, and
minted the first coin. When Eumolpus, king of neighbouring Eleusis, entered Attica with his armies, Erechtheus
defeated him. Eumolpus was killed in the battle, but his
death brought down the wrath of Eumolpus' father, Poseidon, upon Erechtheus, who was killed in his turn.

Erechtheus was mourned by Athena and all Athens.
They buried him on the spot where Poseidon had struck
him down, on the summit of the Acropolis. Later, the

Athenians built a splendid marble temple there and named it the Erechtheum. They dedicated it to Athena, to Poseidon and to Erechtheus, to whom they gave all the honours due to an immortal. From that time onwards, the city of Athens was often called after Erechtheus, too, and from him sprang all the kings of Athens down to the great hero Theseus.

Erechtheus' most lasting gift to his city was the Panathenaea, a great festival in honour of Pallas Athena.

During the festivities, the veil of Athena, woven by the city's most virtuous daughters and borne aloft by its loveliest maidens, was carried with great pomp and ceremony to the Acropolis.

This procession was the highlight of the city's year, and a showpiece for all that Athenians valued and held most beautiful. The most illustrious of its citizens took part: distinguished soldiers and horsemen, the handsomest youths and the loveliest maidens and the bravest and wisest of the old. It was the greatest of honours for an Athenian to be invited to join the procession.

The festival lasted for many days. Athletic events and horse races were held, the epics of Homer were sung, and there were great artistic contests in which singers, dancers and musicians not only from Athens but from all over Greece showed off their skills. The winners of these contests were awarded both olive wreaths and money prizes.

But the Athenians' greatest tribute to their goddess was the Acropolis and its monuments, chief among them the Parthenon, the great temple dedicated to the virgin Athena. This architectural and sculptural miracle is rightly considered to be one of the masterpieces of all times. And fate so decreed that, of all the buildings the world has ever known, the loveliest of all was to be in honour of the goddess who taught men the meaning of beauty, and that the city which chose as its patron the goddess who taught men the meaning of wisdom should become a centre of wisdom for the whole world. There are times, it seems, when there is wisdom even in coincidences.

However wonderful Pallas Athena may seem to us, we should not forget that she was only a product of man's imagination – though one deserving the highest admiration. The works which myth attributes to her were in reality the accomplishments of mortals and the city of Athens rose to fame through the labours of its craftsmen and thinkers. A whole army of shining names, children of Athens and of Greece, stand out among the great of all places and times. In their struggle to achieve goodness and beauty the Athenians won a unique victory – and they did so because they placed above all others the virtues symbolised by the goddess of wisdom: the human spirit, beauty and humanity – that humanity without which beauty loses its radiance and wisdom its power.

Let us close our description of this wonderful goddess with the wise and humane words always spoken by the priest of Athena as he drew the goddess' plough across the sacred courtyard at the foot of the Acropolis:

"Never refuse a stranger water or the warmth of a fire. Never point out any way but the right one. Deny no man a grave. Never kill the ox which draws the plough."

POSEIDON

Poseidon and Athena quarrel over Attica

The boundless seas which sometimes threaten to engulf the stoutest vessel in their rage and at others lap gently against their bows are ruled by earth-shaking Poseidon, brother of Zeus and son of the fearsome Cronus.

Like the seas themselves, this god is sometimes hard-hearted and savage and sometimes gentle and good-willed.

When he is seized by one of his fearful rages he does not care who is on the sea. He thrashes the waters with his trident until the waves rise like mountains and burst in savage fury upon sandy shores or rocky headlands. Woe to any ship that finds itself far from port on these spray-swept seas, for as like as not it will be lost forever. Yet when Poseidon's rage has spent itself, he lays his trident gently upon the surface of the waters and little by little the angry waves calm down. Then trim vessels cleave the seas once more and dolphins follow in their wake, stirring the blue waters in their play.

As a sea-going people, the Greeks held Poseidon in the highest respect and often sought his protection.

Yet, like all the other gods, Poseidon wished to have a single city which owed him special allegiance and to which he could give help and protection in return.

The lord of the sea was especially fond of Attica, where a new city, Cecropia, was being built. The first king of Attica and founder of the new city was Cecrops, son of mother Earth. From the waist downwards he had the body of a snake.

Poseidon came to Attica and found Cecrops on the Acropolis supervising the building of the new city. He asked the king to dedicate the new city to him and to name it Poseidonia in his honour.

"Do as I say, and your city will be ruler of the waves. Your ships will cleave a path through every sea and none will dare to pit their strength against you."

Thus saying, mighty Poseidon brought his trident

crashing down upon the rock, and at the point where the blow had fallen a well appeared, brimming with salty water.

"This is my gift to you," he said. "If you are setting sail for distant parts, kneel and put your ear to the well. If you hear the roaring of the sea, do not leave harbour; for then you will meet great storms in your path and your ships will be swallowed by the waves."

And with these words Poseidon disappeared.

Cecrops had hardly recovered from his surprise when Athena, the goddess of wisdom, suddenly appeared before him. She, too, demanded that the city should bear her name and be called Athens.

"If you carry out my wishes, your city will become the home of beauty and knowledge. Here, art, literature and science will flourish, and from this spot the spirit of freedom will spread out to enlighten the furthest corners of the earth."

So saying, she struck the rock with her spear and from the spot sprang an olive tree, its branches heavy with fruit.

"This is my gift," the goddess declared. "The whole of Attica will be clothed in silvery green by the saplings that spring from this one tree. Its fruit will satisfy your hunger, its oil will give you light and its branches will be a symbol of peace to you and to all men."

Cecrops was delighted with Athena's gift and very much

liked the idea of his city's becoming the world's cultural capital. Yet Poseidon had asked first, and now the king did not know which way to turn.

Suddenly, there was Poseidon once more, and this time furiously angry. He lunged forward to uproot the olive tree, but Athena stepped forward and boldly blocked his path.

This brave stand wounded Poseidon's pride to the quick, and he challenged Athena to a duel. The fearless goddess accepted his challenge.

"Come on, then!" she cried, and taking a few steps backward she grasped her long spear with both hands. Poseidon, too, took up a fighting position, brandishing his fearsome trident in a threatening manner.

The two Olympians were about to come to blows when Zeus himself suddenly appeared before them.

Faced by the ruler of the world, both combatants lowered their weapons, for the word of Zeus was law to them both.

Now Zeus had a great affection for Athena and wished to award the city to her. Yet he knew that Poseidon's terrible temper could not lightly be ignored, and so he decided to summon all the other gods, that the matter might be put to the vote and a decision reached on the spot.

Immediately, all the gods of Olympus gathered on the Acropolis where Cecrops told them exactly what had happened, finally adding:

"Your will shall be respected by me and all the people of Attica. Let temples and statues adorn the Acropolis, and let them be dedicated to the god whom you will choose to be our city's guardian."

After this, the Olympians cast their votes one by one. All the goddesses voted for Athena and all the gods for Poseidon. As Zeus took neither side, Athena won by a single vote. And thus the city was named Athens.

When Poseidon heard the decision his rage was uncontrollable. Whipping up huge waves, he flooded the plain which surrounded the city. The Athenians fled in terror to seek the advice of the oracle and learn what they must do to calm the outraged god.

Pythia told them that Poseidon's anger would only pass if all the women of Athens were punished. They must lose their right to vote and no longer be considered citizens, and their children must henceforth bear their fathers' names, and not their mothers', as they had done till then.

And this is exactly what happened. As a result of the oracle's decision, the last remnants of the old power by which women had once ruled the tribe were finally lost. All this must have happened long ago – perhaps as far back in the past as the founding of Athens itself.

Though Poseidon had lost the new city to Athena, the people of Athens did honour to him on the Acropolis as well as to their patron goddess, and at Cape Sounion they

built him a splendid temple. In return, the sea god was
generous with his help. Athens became a great sea power,
and Poseidon's well on the Acropolis was a gift which the
Athenians kept and found useful on many occasions.

To this very day there is a well on the Acropolis which
is said to be the same one that Poseidon opened with a blow
of his trident. When the wind is in the South, a hollow roar
can be heard from its depths, like the distant thunder of a
storm-tossed sea.

Now that Poseidon had lost Attica, he turned his attention elsewhere. His first choice was Argos, but there he
found himself face to face with Hera, who also wished to
have the city under her protection. The other gods were
again called upon to try the case, but before doing so they
made Poseidon promise that if the vote went against him
and the city were not given into his keeping, he would not
do as he had with Athens. Poseidon gave his word.

Again the gods decided against him and again Poseidon's rage was indescribable. But as he had promised not
to repeat the watery destruction he had wreaked on the
Athenians, he vented his anger in cunning and did just the
opposite: he dried up all the wells. Not until the people of
Argos had built a temple to the god of the sea were they
finally able to pacify him.

After Argos, Poseidon tried to gain a foothold in other
regions but he was obliged in turn to cede Aegina to Zeus,

Delphi to Apollo and Naxos to Dionysus, and it was not until he challenged Helios, the sun god, for the city of Corinth that luck began to smile upon him.

This time it was Briareus, son of Uranus, who entered the arena as a judge, and he played his role with tact and wisdom, giving the upper fortress of Acrocorinth to Helios and Corinth itself and the Isthmus to Poseidon, who was satisfied at last.

The people of Corinth showered honours upon the god of the sea. One of Greece's most renowned festivals was the Isthmian Games, famous for their athletic and artistic contests and second in reputation only to the Olympic Games themselves. On the sacred site where the games were held rose a splendid temple dedicated to the god of the sea. Within it there stood a magnificent statue in Poseidon's likeness, which showed him standing erect and grasping his fearsome trident, his lovely bride Amphitrite seated at his side.

Poseidon and Amphitrite

Mighty Poseidon had taken Amphitrite to be his wife after he had snatched her from her father, the renowned seer Nereus. This old sea god had fifty daughters, the Nereids, among whom were Thetis, the mother of Achilles and, of course, Amphitrite, who loved her old father deeply for his kindness and understanding. Indeed, so great was Amphitrite's love for Nereus that she wished to remain unmarried and stay with him for ever.

But one day, on the shores of the isle of Naxos, Poseidon saw her dancing with her sisters the Nereids and fell in love with her. Amphitrite, however, was so terrified when she saw him that she ran to hide at the very ends of the earth, where the mighty titan Atlas bears all the heavens upon his shoulders.

Poseidon searched and searched for the lovely Nereid, but in vain. In despair, he vented his disappointment upon the blue sea, lashing it into foam with his fearsome trident. Month after month went by, and still the sea rose in mountainous waves lashed by savage spray. Finally, when it seemed that calm would never again return to the face of the waters, mighty Zeus sent his brother Poseidon a dolphin which revealed Amphitrite's hiding-place to the ruler of the seas. Poseidon immediately went there, found Nereus' daughter and took her for his wife — and so at last the waves dropped and the sea was calm once more.

Now Amphitrite lived in a majestic sapphire palace deep beneath the waves. Far above, storms might lash the surface but down there all was forever still and peaceful. Hosts of sea nymphs were at Amphitrite's call and served her every wish.

Drawn by four immortal horses, she would often thunder

over the waves in a chariot, at the side of her husband, Poseidon the earth-shaker.

At their passing the waves would part, the seabirds wheel joyfully about them and the dolphins frolic in the blue waters.

The immortal pair were often accompanied by a host of sea deities. Among them were the Nereids, Amphitrite's sisters, and their father Nereus, the great seer of the oceans who did not know what a lie was and only revealed the truth to men. Among them, too, was their son Triton, who was a great sea god in his own right. When he blew upon his horns they rang out with a great blast and caused fearful storms. There, too, was old Proteus who never wished to reveal his seer's knowledge and would escape his questioners by turning himself into a snake, a lion, to fire, to water, or whatever he wished; and Glaucus, who started life as a humble fisherman and had become a sea god and a soothsayer. For all his change of fortunes he had stayed as modest and generous as when he was a mortal. He loved sailors and fishermen and helped them whenever he saw danger threatening.

Poseidon fathered many children, not only with Amphitrite but with other women, too. However, most of his offspring were monsters and brought men nothing but ill-fortune. Not that this should strike us as strange, for we should never forget that Poseidon was the god of the sea, and the sea has always brought men bitter experiences. Its call draws the bold like a magnet, yet how often are brave seafarers sucked down beneath its foaming waves! How often are the hopes and dreams of men shattered like the wreckage that strews its waters, and those who long for the return of loved ones filled with despair!

Yet most of the time the god of the seas is a protector of ships, and then they set their sails to a fair wind and make a safe and speedy voyage.

As well as being ruler of the waves, Poseidon, true Greek god that he is, also protects the land of his birth from its enemies.

Thus legend has it that he thrust his trident into the sea and stirred up waves as high as mountains to wreck the Persian fleet upon the rocky shores of Athos when Xerxes sailed to invade Greece. And at the battle of Salamis it is said that Poseidon himself brought confusion upon the Persians and helped the Greeks to shatter them.

People even used to say that many bold seafarers were sons of Poseidon. The most famous of them all was Byzas, who founded Byzantium.

Ancaeus

Another of his sons, Ancaeus, founded the city of Samos, and there is a legend about him which is worth recounting.

Ancaeus was a harsh and ruthless ruler who treated his slaves with great severity. Once, he was planting a vineyard. To get the job finished more quickly he forced his slaves to work hard – so hard that one of them, bolder than the rest, plucked up his courage and reminded his master of the proverb:

"Never kill the ox that draws the plough."

"And what do you mean by that?" roared Ancaeus.

"Just what the proverb says, master. You do wrong to behave like this towards those who toil so that you may enjoy wealth and power. And let me tell you something else: your haste to finish the task is all in vain, for you will never taste the wine from this vineyard."

Ancaeus was beside himself with rage, yet he said nothing, for his fear was even greater than his anger. Many men had the power of prophecy, and sometimes it was stronger in a slave than in a free man.

Three years went by. The vines became heavy with grapes, their juice was pressed and fermented, and soon the time came to open the vats and taste the wine.

Then Ancaeus took a cup and called the slave who had spoken those words to him three years before.

"Come here, you!" he cried, "and fill my cup with wine." Without a word, the slave did as Ancaeus had commanded him.

"Fill cups for everybody," he went on, "and fill one for yourself as well." When the drinks had all been poured, Ancaeus lifted his cup aloft and said sneeringly to the slave:

"Remember what you told me once? Come, my friend — to your health!"

"Do not think I wish you ill, master," the slave replied, "but, alas, there's many a slip twixt the cup and the lip."

At that moment terrified voices were heard crying:

"A wild boar! A wild boar is uprooting the vineyard!"

Putting down his cup instantly, Ancaeus ran to see what was happening and the wild boar charged and killed him.

When Poseidon learned of the evil ending the fates had written for his son his rage was ungovernable. The furious sea swelled to mountainous heights. All who found themselves in open waters were in mortal danger and many seafarers were lost for ever. The waves broke in frenzy upon the rocks, hurling spray into the heavens. It was a long time before Poseidon's rage subsided and the sea fell calm once more.

HESTIA

A humble goddess

Of all the gods and goddesses, says that great poet Homer, there was none that mortal men loved and respected more than Hestia.

Hestia was a humble goddess. No impressive myths have been woven about her name. She was simple and unassuming; no exciting adventures befell her and no great feats ever crowned her with glory.

And yet men adored her above all others. What other goddess could boast an altar in every house, lit with an undying flame? She it was whom men begged to bless their

food when they sat to table and she to whom they gave
thanks when they rose after each meal. Even when a sacrifice was made to another god, the sacrificial hymn always
began with a reference to her name and the fat that dripped
from every sacrifice was hers by right.

Why should such a humble goddess have been held in so
great honour? The answer is simple: because Hestia was
the goddess of the home and of its undying fire.

Was this alone enough to make her such a beloved figure? Yes, it was enough. But to understand why, we shall
have to go on a journey – no ordinary journey but one back
into the past. Buckling on the wings of fantasy we must fly
back across those dim and distant years until, choosing a
winter evening, we secretly enter the humble dwelling of a
family of simple working folk.

The way they live will come as a surprise, for their
house is nothing more than a rough, square room. In the
middle there is a low hearth. This is the altar we mentioned
earlier. Indeed, it even bears the name of the goddess and is
called the "hestia." On it, a log fire is burning brightly. In
the middle of the ceiling there is a hole for the smoke to
escape. Food is cooking over the fire, watched over by the
mother. Now she takes the pot from the flames and opens
it. A rich odour of tasty soup spreads throughout the room.
The whole family is now gathered around the hearth.
Basking in the warmth of the flames they relax after a long,

hard day's work in the fields. Here, around the fire, the children seek out the father's caress, the grandfather's knee. Here, their mother surrounds them with love as she serves out wheaten bread and steaming soup.

And we, who entered the house unobserved, have seen all we need to know to answer our question and say why it was that mortals so adored Hestia, goddess of their hearth and home.

We have all understood by now, of course, that Hestia was worshipped so sincerely because men loved the warmth of the family circle, peace and life itself. Men loved the humble gods better than the proud, for they were closer to them.

Hestia was the elder sister of Zeus and daughter of the fearsome Cronus. Like Athena and Artemis, she was a virgin goddess. Her only desire was to warm the hearts of men, and the fire that burnt in every home symbolised that warming influence. Its flames must never be allowed to die in the hearth, for if they did, great evil would befall the house. Moreover, in those early days it was no easy matter to get a fire alight and so it was hardly an exaggeration to call a dead fire a terrible misfortune.

Thus the fire in the hearth was kept burning from generation to generation. When the children grew up and married, they took burning coals from their father's house to light the fire in their new home. The flame was passed on from father to son, keeping its light and warmth for hundreds and even thousands of years. For this reason it was called the ancestral hearth, and men were ready to die in its defence when danger threatened, for in doing so they were defending their children, their wives, their old folks and their very homes.

However, it was not only in houses that such fires were kept burning. In every city there was a public building called the "prytaneion". In the centre of its largest chamber stood an altar to the goddess Hestia, where an eternal flame was kept alight. When people from a city left to found colonies in distant lands, they carried with them fire from that altar for the new altar in the city which they would build. Its flame would remind them forever of the sacred bond between the new city and the old, and it symbolised the unquenchable longing of the exile for his homeland.

Being a family goddess, Hestia loved and protected children. It was to her care that Alcestis left her children before she died. But that myth, so rich in humanity and self-sacrifice, we shall speak about in a later book when we come to tell of Heracles.

TABLE OF CONTENTS

Aphrodite

Apollo

Hermes

Demeter

Menelaos Stephanides, the author of 'Greek Mythology', originally studied economics but has spent the last twenty-five years in the completion of this eight-volume series, in the course of which he has acquired an expert knowledge of the myths of the ancient Greek world. His aim has been not only to produce a complete and accurate work, but above all, as he has often said, one which the reader would be reluctant to put down. To this end he has remoulded and reworked the materials he has amassed in his research, and the warmth with which successive volumes have been received since the first was published in 1977 is a clear measure of the extent to which he has succeeded. The originality of his approach lies in the emphasis he places on moral values not evident in earlier versions and in the clarification of mythological themes which till now have gone unnoticed. For example, this is the only mythology so far published in which the chronology of the myths is clearly defined, and the last volume of the series, which brings the reader to the swan-song of the age of myth, is perhaps its crowning glory.

In 1989, Menelaos Stephanides was awarded by the Pier Paolo Vergerio European Prizes of the University of Padua. His 'Greek Mythology' has been translated into many languages.

The artist and illustrator Yannis Stephanides, more than 250 of whose pencil drawings adorn the eight volumes of the 'Greek Mythology' series, studied painting at the School of Fine Arts in Athens. He has made his name, both in Greece and abroad, chiefly as a book illustrator, a field to which he has devoted himself almost exclusively for more than thirty years. Among his major achievements are the more than five hundred colour illustrations he created for the 18-volume children's edition of 'Greek Mythology', a landmark in publications for young people which has been translated into ten foreign languages.

Yannis Stephanides' work has been displayed at many painting and illustration exhibitions in Athens and at international venues.

He was awarded by the Pier Paolo Vergerio European Prizes for book illustrations of the University of Padua in 1989 and in 1998 he gained an award from the Greek section of IBBY, the International Organization for Books for Young People. He also won an "excellent" award at the International Print Biennale 2000 in Quindao, China.

Since 1995 he has also made a name for himself as an author, illustrating his own books.

GREEK MYTHOLOGY SERIES

AN INDEX OF ALL NAMES
appearing in this Greek Mythology series
is included in volume 4: Theseus - Perseus